P9-EAN-913

DATE DUE

DE 20 '96	NO 1 07		
MR '97	OC 2 2 08		
JY 1 '97	MR 1 7 '09		
JY 14 '97			
DE 9 '97			
BE 3 '98			
MY 27 '99			
NO 29 99			
MR 30 01			
MY 16 07			
OC 22 '03			
DE 10 03			
MR 29 04			
MR 23 05			
SE 7 06			
AG 3 06			
OC 3 06			

DEMCO 38-296

Search, Seizure, and Privacy

Exploring the Constitution Series

by Darien A. McWhirter

The Separation of Church and State
Freedom of Speech, Press, and Assembly
Search, Seizure, and Privacy
Equal Protection

Search, Seizure, and Privacy

by
Darien A. McWhirter

Exploring the Constitution Series
Darien A. McWhirter, Series Editor

Oryx Press

1994

The rare Arabian Oryx is believed to have inspired the myth of the unicorn. This desert antelope became virtually extinct in the early 1960s. At that time several groups of international conservationists arranged to have 9 animals sent to the Phoenix Zoo to be the nucleus of a captive breeding herd. Today the Oryx population is over 800 and nearly 400 have been returned to reserves in the Middle East.

© 1994 by Darien A. McWhirter
Published by The Oryx Press
4041 North Central at Indian School Road
Phoenix, Arizona 85012-3397

Published simultaneously in Canada
Printed and Bound in the United States of America

♾ The paper used in this publication meets the minimum requirements of American National Standard for Information Science—Permanence of Paper for Printed Library Materials, ANSI Z39.48, 1984

This publication is designed to provide accurate and authoritative information in regard to the subject matter covered. It is sold with the understanding that the publisher is not engaged in rendering legal, accounting, or other professional services. If legal advice or other expert assistance is required, the services of a competent professional should be sought.
From a Declaration of Principles jointly adopted by a Committee of the American Bar Association and the Committee of Publishers.

Library of Congress Cataloging-in-Publication Data

McWhirter, Darien A. (Darien Auburn)
  Search, seizure, and privacy/ by Darien A. McWhirter.
    p. cm.—(Exploring the Constitution series)
Includes bibliographical references and index.
ISBN 0-89774-854-9
  1. Searches and seizures—United States—Cases. 2. Privacy, Right of—United States—Cases. [1. Searches and seizures—History. 2. Privacy, Right of—History. 3. United States—Constitutional law—Amendments—4th—History.] I. Title. II. Series.
KF9630.A7M36 1994
345.73'0522'02634—dc20
[347.30552202634]   94-27882
                                      CIP
                                      AC

CONTENTS

❀ ❀ ❀ ❀ ❀ ❀ ❀ ❀

SERIES STATEMENT

❋ ❋ ❋ ❋ ❋ ❋ ❋ ❋

The Constitution of the United States is one of the most important documents ever written, but it is not just of historical interest. Over two centuries after its adoption, the Constitution continues to influence the lives of everyone in the United States. Many of the most divisive social issues, from abortion to free speech, have been and are being resolved by the U.S. Supreme Court through interpretation of the U.S. Constitution.

Yet much of what has been written about these Supreme Court decisions and the Constitution itself has served only to confuse people who would like to understand exactly what the Court has ruled and exactly what the Constitution means. So much of the discussion revolves around what the Constitution *should* mean that what the Constitution actually *does* mean is obscured.

The Exploring the Constitution Series provides a basic introduction to important areas of constitutional law. While the books in this series are appropriate for a general audience, every effort has been made to ensure that they are especially accessible to high school and college students.

Each volume contains a general introduction to a particular constitutional issue combined with excerpts from significant Supreme Court decisions in that area. The text of the Constitution, a chronological listing of the Supreme Court justices, and a glossary of legal terms are included in each volume. Every effort has been made to provide an objective analysis of the Court's interpretation of constitutional issues with an emphasis on how that interpretation has evolved over time.

PREFACE

❋ ❋ ❋ ❋ ❋ ❋ ❋ ❋ ❋

No area of constitutional decision making has generated more difficult decisions for the Court than the area of search and seizure. As the many people who watched O.J. Simpson's preliminary hearing on television in the summer of 1994 learned, search and seizure decisions can be complex and controversial. With decisions that require the Court to balance the rights of citizens to be free from invasions of privacy against the need of law enforcement to catch and prosecute criminals, the Supreme Court has been called upon to state the rules that control how police and other officials at every level of government must act. Issues such as when to invoke the exclusionary rule have kept the Supreme Court busy over the course of many decades.

PURPOSE

While this volume is written for everyone, every effort has been made to make the discussion interesting and accessible to high school and undergraduate college students. Issues and Supreme Court decisions have been chosen with an eye to what students might find interesting. Cases involving schools have been included whenever appropriate.

This volume is intended to be useful both as a reference work and as a supplement to the standard textbook in social studies, history, government, political science, and law courses. The Supreme Court decisions reprinted here were chosen because of their importance and the likelihood that they would stimulate discussion about the issues presented in this volume. Teachers should consider having students read only the actual Court decisions in preparation for class discussion, and then having students read the discussion material following the class discussion.

In addition to the actual texts of some of the most important Supreme Court decisions in this area, this volume provides the reader with discussions that place those decisions into their legal and historical context. While other sources provide either analysis or the text of actual Court decisions, this volume attempts to provide both in a format that will stimulate thinking and provide a general overview to this important area of constitutional law. Reading the discussion as well as the decisions is necessary for anyone who is really interested in understanding how the Supreme Court has interpreted the Fourth Amendment. It is assumed, however, that readers have a general understanding of how the American legal system works and the role of the U.S. Supreme Court in that system.

Other sources have discussed some of the material presented here, but such discussions usually only present one side of the debate. This volume attempts to explain as objectively as possible what the Supreme Court has ruled in this area. Supreme Court decisions are criticized here only if they do not logically follow from earlier decisions, not because they fail to live up to the author's personal beliefs about what the Court should rule in this complex area of constitutional law.

ARRANGEMENT

This volume discusses the major privacy and search and seizure issues that the Supreme Court has addressed. Chapter 2 examines the Court's decisions concerning what is protected by the Fourth Amendment. Chapter 3 examines the complex area of when police and other government officials may search buildings such as homes and businesses. Chapter 4 looks at when police may search and seize people while they are out in public. Chapter 5 explores the difficult area of when automobiles and baggage may be searched and seized. Chapter 6 traces the history and development of the exclusionary rule. Chapter 7 examines the right to privacy beyond search and seizure, such as the right to have an abortion.

Each of the six substantive chapters (2 through 7) is divided into three parts. The first part, "Discussion," provides an overview of the important Supreme Court decisions in a particular area to show the development of the Supreme Court's thinking over time. Each of the substantive chapters also contains excerpts from the text of Supreme Court decisions that illustrate the major issues under discussion and the logic behind the Court's thinking in each area. Discussion questions at the end of each of these chapters are intended to stimulate both thought and discussion.

The table of cases provides references to all of the Supreme Court decisions discussed in the text. Anyone wishing to read the actual decisions may find them by showing the reference to a librarian in a library that contains the Supreme Court's decisions. The citation 374 U.S. 203 (1963), for example, tells us that the decision was made in 1963, and that the text of the decision is contained in volume 374 of the United States Reports at page 203.

The glossary is included to provide a ready reference, but readers may wish to research some of the terms further. Not every term found in the glossary will be found in each volume of this series.

This volume includes two appendixes. Appendix A contains the complete text of the Constitution. Appendix B contains a chronological listing of all the justices who have sat on the U.S. Supreme Court.

When James Madison wrote the first draft of what would become the Fourth Amendment, he acknowledged the central place the right to be free from unreasonable searches and seizures had in the minds of those who fought and won the American Revolution. Many consider the right to be free of unreasonable searches and seizures to have been the most difficult right for the Supreme Court to interpret over the course of the twentieth century. It is only by reading the Court's actual decisions and understanding the legal and historical context of those decisions that any citizen can begin to understand what the law is in this area and why it is what it is. It is to that end that this volume was written and it is to the education of those citizens that this volume is dedicated.

Darien A. McWhirter
San Jose, California
August 1994

TABLE OF CASES
CITED IN THE TEXT

❖ ❖ ❖ ❖ ❖ ❖ ❖ ❖

CHAPTER
one
* * * * * * * * *

Introduction

Search and seizure law is drawn primarily from the Fourth Amendment, which has been called the most ambiguous of the 10 amendments that make up the Bill of Rights. Over time, the Supreme Court has come to see the protection of property and privacy as the main purpose of the Fourth Amendment. However, the Court has concluded that the amendment does not protect *all* property interests or apply to *all* situations where people might wish to protect their privacy. To understand how the Court reached its interpretation of the Fourth Amendment requires a trip into history.

In England and its American colonies in the late 1700s, popular feeling ran high against the use of what were called "general warrants" and "writs of assistance." These were government documents police and customs officers used as licenses to search any building or home. The warrants and writs were seldom used to search for evidence of what today we would call common crime. Instead, searches were usually conducted to find traitorous writings against the king of England or smuggled goods that legally belonged to the king because customs duties had not been paid. After the American Revolution, the English Parliament passed statutes to limit the use of these kinds of warrants and writs in England.

It is important to understand the legal context of the time. Under English common law, the warrant served one main function. If government officials invaded private property without a good reason, they could be sued personally for trespassing. If they had a warrant, they were immune from such lawsuits. General warrants authorizing government officials to go anywhere gave them complete immunity from such suits and the power to enter any piece of private property to carry out a search.

JAMES OTIS'S ARGUMENT

In the second half of the eighteenth century in what would become the United States, general warrants and writs of assistance were routinely used to authorize customs officials to search any home or business for smuggled goods. In 1761 James Otis, Jr., a famous attorney representing 63 Boston merchants, sued customs officials in an effort to stop the use of such writs. James Otis's argument lasted five hours and we do not know everything he said, but he did say that "A man's house is his castle; and whilst he is quiet, he is as well guarded as a prince in his castle." He lost the case, but many believe the resentment against the use of these writs was a major cause of the American Revolution.

A young John Adams was in the courtroom when James Otis made his argument that the private property of the colonists deserved to be respected. John Adams later wrote that he left the courtroom determined to bring an end to such abuses and that, in his opinion, the American Revolution really began with that lawsuit.

WRITING THE FOURTH AMENDMENT

After the successful end of the American Revolution, the new United States struggled to operate as a loose confederation. When that failed, a Constitution was drafted. Many states objected to the Constitution as it was first proposed, saying they would not approve a constitution that did not include a bill of rights. These states approved the Constitution only after assurances that a bill of rights would soon be added. When the first Congress assembled after the Constitution was adopted, James Madison proposed the addition of 12 amendments. The 10 that were ultimately passed by Congress and ratified by the states became the Bill of Rights.

There was little debate about the scope and meaning of the Fourth Amendment in Congress. James Madison proposed that the amendment read:

> The rights of the people to be secured in their persons, their houses, their papers, and their other property, from all unreasonable searches and seizures, shall not be violated by warrants issued without probable cause, supported by oath or affirmation, or not particularly describing the places to be searched, or the persons or things to be seized.

The amendment as passed by Congress and ratified by the states reads:

> The right of the people to be secure in their persons, houses, papers, and effects, against unreasonable searches and seizures, shall not be violated,

and no Warrants shall issue, but upon probable cause, supported by Oath or affirmation, and particularly describing the place to be searched, and the persons or things to be seized.

The final version was very similar to Madison's original proposal, and the changes seem to have been made primarily to make the amendment read better rather than to alter the intended meaning. The only important changes Congress made to Madison's draft were the change of "their other property" to "effects" and the change of "or" to "and." Why was Madison's phrase "other property" changed to "effects"? Did Congress think it was expanding the scope of the amendment with this change or contracting it?

Where Madison had said that the warrant must either describe the places to be searched "or" the persons or things to be seized, the final version said that the warrant must describe the place to be searched "and" the persons or things to be seized. What does this change suggest about the intent of Congress? One might argue that Madison imagined that a warrant would be needed if either a place was to be searched "or" a person or thing was to be seized, while Congress thought that a warrant would be needed if both a place was to be searched and a person or thing was to be seized. Other interpretations are just as reasonable.

The ambiguity of the amendment raises many questions. When is a warrant required? Is a warrant only needed to search a house or building, or is it needed whenever anyone or anything is to be searched or seized, even out on the public street? It could be argued that the change from "or" to "and" meant that only searches and seizures on private property were considered to need a warrant but we have no record from the congressional debate to support that interpretation. Are there situations where a warrant is not needed to search or seize people or property, and, if so, what is needed in those circumstances? The amendment says that it protects "persons, houses, papers, and effects." What about apartments or hotel rooms? The amendment could have said "home" instead of "house," so did Congress intend that it would only apply to houses? What about businesses and warehouses? We know that James Otis was unhappy because businesses and warehouses had been searched for smuggled goods with the authority of a general warrant. Why didn't Congress put "place of business" on the list? Was the amendment intended only to protect private real estate from trespass, or was Congress concerned with other issues, such as protecting personal privacy?

All of these questions were left up to the U.S. Supreme Court to answer, and the Court did not begin to answer them until 1886 when it handed down its first decision interpreting the Fourth Amendment. From that time to the present the Court has found that the usual methods of constitutional interpretation provide little guidance in this area.

CONSTITUTIONAL DECISION MAKING

The Supreme Court has developed a number of approaches to use in making decisions about constitutional provisions. The justices may use one, or more than one, approach in any one case. First, they may try to figure out what the authors of a particular provision had in mind when they wrote it. This approach is difficult to use to interpret the Bill of Rights. The amendments that make up the Bill of Rights were voted on not only by Congress but also by the many state legislatures, and it is not easy to determine what all of those people had in mind when they cast their votes.

Second, constitutional decision making often involves drawing a line. The Court decides that one type of behavior is protected from governmental interference by a particular provision of the Bill of Rights and another type of behavior is not.

Third, the Court may try to balance governmental goals against individual rights. In evaluating a case, the Court must weigh the importance of the goals government is trying to achieve by passing a particular law or by engaging in a particular action against the damage the law or action appears to do to the individual rights of citizens. Often the Supreme Court asks how "compelling" is the goal government is trying to achieve. Then the Court tries to balance that against the importance of the right that is being infringed upon.

Although the Supreme Court has tried to use all three decision-making approaches in interpreting the Fourth Amendment, decision making has not been easy in this area. There was little debate about the Fourth Amendment on the floor of the House and Senate, so it is difficult to know what the people who wrote the amendment had in mind. The Supreme Court has assumed that they certainly had James Otis in mind, because no other piece of pre-Revolutionary American history has been quoted as often by the Court as the story of James Otis and the impact his lawsuit had on young John Adams. But what does that tell us? Apparently, Congress at least intended the Fourth Amendment to prevent the searching of businesses and warehouses without a specific, as opposed to a general, warrant.

In trying to draw a line between what the Fourth Amendment does and does not protect, the Court has run into some problems. The Fourth Amendment only talks about "persons, houses, papers, and effects." Does that mean it does not apply to the search of an automobile? After all, there were wagons and carriages at the time the amendment was written and Congress could have added "wagons" to the list. How important is it that Congress did not? Is it unreasonable to expect an exhaustive list in a constitutional amendment which is by its very nature intended to be short and to express principles rather than details?

What about balancing? That has not been an easy approach either. When weighed against the government's need to search for smuggled goods, the rights of the people seem to tip the scale. But when the government needs to search for a murderer, that need tips the balance the other way. The Court cannot make different rules for different types of crimes, however, because that would be too complex and impossible for lawyers and judges to enforce.

Since 1886, when the Supreme Court first took up the question of the meaning of the Fourth Amendment, the makeup of the Court has changed significantly.

THE SUPREME COURT OVER TIME

Generally people divide the history of the Supreme Court into three major eras: before the Civil War, between the Civil War and the Great Depression, and the modern era. The modern era can be broken up further into the New Deal Court (1941–53), the Warren Court (1953–69), the Burger Court (1969–86), and the Rehnquist Court (1986–present).

Pre-Civil War to the Great Depression

Before the Civil War the Supreme Court spent very little time on the meaning of the Bill of Rights. The Court decided that the Bill of Rights restricted only the federal government. State and local governments were free to do whatever they wanted, limited only by the bills of rights contained in state constitutions. Most of the governmental activities that touched people's lives were carried on by state governments, not by the federal government.

The Civil War was a great turning point in American history. With the victory of the Union army, two fundamental questions that had not been answered by the Constitution were well on their way to resolution. These were the question of the extent of the federal government's power to control the states and the question of slavery. After the Civil War, in the partnership between the states and the federal government, the federal government would be the more powerful partner, and slavery would be abolished in the United States. The Thirteenth, Fourteenth, and Fifteenth Amendments were then passed to make it clear to future generations which side had won the Civil War and what should follow from that victory.

- The Thirteenth Amendment outlawed slavery.
- The Fourteenth Amendment guaranteed the equal protection of the law to everyone and provided that life, liberty, or property could only be taken following due process of law.
- The Fifteenth Amendment guaranteed the right to vote to the former slaves.

Between the Civil War and the Great Depression, the Supreme Court struggled to decide what these three amendments actually meant; the key question for the Court was the meaning of the Fourteenth Amendment. The Court decided that the amendment protected basic liberties of all Americans from infringement by state and local governments, but this raised another difficult question: What were the basic liberties that were protected? Between the Civil War and the Great Depression, the Court refused to be specific in answering this question. The Court simply took each case as it came and decided whether or not the freedoms involved were important enough to protect with the Fourteenth Amendment.

Critics of the Court argued that the members of the Court were simply using the Fourteenth Amendment as an excuse to overturn laws passed by the state legislatures because a majority of the justices did not agree with the laws, not because the laws violated any particular right. From the 1880s to the 1930s, 200 statutes were overturned by the Court. Most of these statutes attempted to regulate industry. For example, the Court overturned a New York law that limited bakers to a 60-hour workweek. Other laws declared unconstitutional had attempted to protect a worker's right to join a labor union. While the Court argued that it was protecting the right of workers to work more than 60 hours a week and to not join labor unions, critics argued that the Court was mainly protecting the right of employers to exploit their employees.

The Modern Era

Beginning in the 1930s, the Court began to move away from this expansive idea and to develop the concept that the Fourteenth Amendment actually made most of the federal Bill of Rights applicable to state and local governments. This countered the critics and enabled the Court to give real substance to the Fourteenth Amendment's command that everyone should be able to enjoy liberty in the United States.

The composition of the Court was changing. Between the Civil War and the Great Depression the Court was primarily made up of conservative

Republicans. By 1941 eight of the justices were liberal Democrats appointed by President Roosevelt. What had been a conservative court dominated by Republicans became a liberal court dominated by Democrats, the New Deal Court. As a practical matter this meant that the Court spent less time trying to protect business from government and more time trying to protect the rights of individuals and minority groups.

In 1953 President Eisenhower appointed Earl Warren as chief justice of the Supreme Court, and in 1956 Eisenhower appointed William Brennan associate justice. These two justices turned out to be as concerned with the rights of individuals and minorities as the New Deal Court had been. The period from 1953 to 1969 is known as the Warren era in Supreme Court history, and many difficult issues concerning the meaning of the Bill of Rights and the relative power of the state and federal governments were decided by the Warren Court.

In 1969 President Nixon appointed Warren Burger as chief justice; Burger was replaced by William Rehnquist in 1986. During this period, through the Burger Court and the Rehnquist Court, the Supreme Court is generally considered to have moved in a more conservative direction. That does not mean that the decisions of the New Deal and Warren Courts were simply overturned—far from it—but the tone and direction of the Court did change. The interests of the state and federal government were given greater emphasis, along with the needs of business.

Although the direction of the Court may change over time with the addition of new justices, the Court is limited by the doctrine of *stare decisis*. This is a Latin phrase meaning "the decision must stand." In the U.S. legal system it means that generally a past decision of the Supreme Court will not be overturned except under exceptional circumstances.

In the area of search and seizure law, the political and ideological affiliation of the justices has been a factor in helping to determine how they vote. For example, during the 1920s and 1930s the more liberal justices often found themselves dissenting from the conservative majority and arguing in favor of more deference to the right of the people to be free from unreasonable searches and seizures. At the same time, even during periods of dominance by either liberal Democrats (the 1940s) or conservative Republicans (the 1980s), there has been a great deal of disagreement about how far the protection against unreasonable searches and seizures should go.

The news media has made more of these ideological differences than is justified by the actual decisions. The conservative Republican Court handed down decisions in 1886 and 1914 that were very expansive in their desire to protect people from unreasonable searches and seizures. It could be argued that the conservative justices in the 1920s were just as untrue to these early decisions as the Warren Court was untrue to the decisions handed down in the 1920s. Also, many of the decisions that were later modified or overturned were modified or overturned by the same group of justices that had handed them down in the first place. The Warren Court modified some of its early rulings in this area, and the Burger Court did the same thing. Anyone who suggests that the changes in the Court's opinions in the area of search and seizure were simply the result of changes in the makeup of the Court is being very misleading. Liberal Democrats have rejected past opinions by liberal Democrats and conservative Republicans have rejected past opinions by conservative Republicans.

THE SOCIAL DEBATE AND THE EXCLUSIONARY RULE

The question of how much the Fourth Amendment should limit the right of the police to search for evidence of criminal activity has stirred much debate. The Supreme Court did not really decide until 1961 that the Fourteenth Amendment made the Fourth Amendment applicable to the states. That year, in the case of *Mapp v. Ohio* (see p. 107), the Court decided not only that the Fourth Amendment was applicable to the states but also that it required judges at all levels of government to make use of the exclusionary rule. The exclusionary rule simply states that if something has been seized by the police in violation of the Fourth Amendment, it cannot be used as evidence against the person whose rights were violated. Because of the exclusionary rule, judges faced with convicted murderers and robbers would often have to let them go free because the evidence used to convict them had been obtained in a way that violated the Fourth Amendment. Throughout the 1960s and into the 1970s, the press and many political leaders protested against this result. It was common for the press to say that a murderer was going free because of a "legal technicality." Headlines in magazines and newspapers expressed the opinion that the Supreme Court had "handcuffed" the police and that lawlessness was the direct result. The Supreme Court responded that the dictates of the Fourth Amendment amounted to more than a legal technicality—they were part of the Bill of Rights. One criticism leveled at the Court's decisions seemed legitimate: the Court's decisions in the area of search and seizure were unclear and left the police confused about what they could and could not do in many situations.

During the 1967–68 school year, the national high school debate topic was "Resolved, that Congress shall establish a uniform code of criminal investigation procedure." In high school debates, student debate teams must be prepared to argue both sides of the resolution and to back up their argument with facts and quotations from recognized authorities on the subject. High school students throughout the country combed the magazines and books that had been published during the 1960s to marshal every argument against the current state of the law on search and seizure. The winning affirmative case was based on the issue of confusion. The debaters could muster dozens of experts who expressed the opinion that police were confused about what they could or could not do in the area of search and seizure, and about when they needed a warrant. They did not know when they needed probable cause without a warrant and when they could simply search without either probable cause or a warrant. This confusion, it was argued, could only be cleared up if Congress stepped in and passed a uniform code of criminal investigation procedure that would clear up these problems. The negative case that stood up the best was that Congress simply did not have the power to write a code interpreting the Bill of Rights; only the Supreme Court had the final word on what the Fourth Amendment meant. It would be up to the Court to get out of the mess it had created for itself and for the society it served. In the real world Congress did not even try to deal with this issue. It would indeed be up to the Supreme Court to clear up the confusion.

In 1966 the Court eliminated a great deal of confusion about confessions. The Fifth Amendment states that people cannot be compelled to testify against themselves. The Court ruled early on that this meant confessions could not be obtained through the use of violence and physical coercion. The police then came up with more sophisticated methods of eliciting confessions that involved the use of psychological manipulation. The Supreme Court's 1966 decision in *Miranda v. Arizona*, one of its most famous rulings, dealt with this issue. The case involved a confession that might have been the result of psychological manipulation but was clearly not the result of physical violence. The Court ruled that from that time forward police wishing to question a person who had been taken into custody could do so, and could use psychological manipulation short of physical violence, but first they would have to "read the person his rights." The Court spelled out what would have to be said. Every police officer in the United States soon had a note card in his or her pocket with the following words:

> You have the right to remain silent. If you give up that right anything you say can and will be used against you in a court of law. You have a right to an attorney and to have your attorney present during questioning. If you cannot afford an attorney one will be appointed for you. Do you understand your rights?

Suddenly the confusion was over. If police read people in custody their rights and did not use physical violence against them, then the confessions would not be thrown out by the Supreme Court. If the police did not read people in custody their rights, they risked having the confessions thrown out by a federal judge. While many people criticized this ruling, the police did not because it provided them with clear guidance concerning what they could do in the area of confessions. Most children in the United States know what the Miranda warning is by the time they are seven or eight years old because they have heard it many times on television cop shows.

Throughout the 1970s and 1980s and into the 1990s, the Supreme Court searched for simple, straightforward rules in the area of search and seizure that, like the Miranda decision, would provide a reasonable level of protection for people's rights and at the same time not impede law enforcement too much. Writing these rules would be a long and difficult task for the Supreme Court.

CONSENT AND STANDING

One area of the law of search and seizure that confuses many people concerns the doctrines of consent and standing. The Supreme Court has always said that people may consent to give up their constitutional rights as long as they have not been forced to do so. Whenever people confess to crimes, they are giving up their right to refuse to testify against themselves. They have consented to give up that right. The same applies to the Fourth Amendment. If a person gives the police permission to search his or her own home, then the search will not violate the Constitution. This can get complicated, however, because more than one person may have control over an area the police wish to search. For example, if three people rent a house together, they each have the right to consent to a search of the entire house. They each have control over the house and the power to allow anyone into the house, including the police. If one of the roommates is found to possess illegal drugs, he or she cannot complain if another roommate consented to the search. The roommate had the power to consent to the search and did just that.

People unfamiliar with the legal system may also find the concept of standing complicated. Generally, people must have had their own rights violated before they can object in court. The justification for this is that if the person who really suffered is not willing to take the case to Court, why should a busy legal system bother with the case? In the area of search and seizure, the issue of standing usually comes up when the police have violated the Fourth Amendment and searched one person's house only to find evidence that another person is guilty of a crime. Let's say that the police have searched Bill's house in violation of the Fourth Amendment and have found evidence that Fred, who is not living in Bill's house, is guilty of a crime. The police can use the evidence against Fred and Fred has no legal complaint. It was Bill's rights that were violated, not Fred's. If the police tried to use the evidence against Bill he could object and the exclusionary rule would keep the evidence out of court.

The issues of consent and standing can become complex. Often the question is whether or not the person, free of coercion by the police, consented to a search. Also, with the issue of standing, it is not always clear when someone has a legal right to complain about the actions of the police. A houseguest who is temporarily staying with a friend has standing to complain about a search of the house while a guest there but not when he or she is no longer a guest.

While these concepts may seem strange, they go back centuries in English common law and have been brought into U.S. constitutional law by the Supreme Court.

CONCLUSION

This book discusses a difficult and divisive area of constitutional decision making, the right to be free from unreasonable searches and seizures. Those of us who approach the issue today have the benefit of both hindsight and over a century of Supreme Court decisions on the subject. We can see what questions and problems have resulted from particular decisions that could not have been anticipated by the justices who made those decisions.

No matter what a person's opinions are concerning the proper balance between the need for effective law enforcement and the right to be free from unreasonable searches and seizures, it is important to understand what the Court has ruled in this area and why. Disagreement based on ignorance is worthless. Reasoned argument based on understanding and facts is the most powerful weapon anyone can wield in a free society.

CHAPTER
two

❖ ❖ ❖ ❖ ❖ ❖ ❖ ❖

Protecting Property and Privacy

•••••••••••••••••••••••••••••••••••• **DISCUSSION** ••••••••••••••••••••••••••••••••

The fundamental task in interpreting any provision of the Bill of Rights is to determine exactly what the particular amendment protects. In cases involving the Fourth Amendment, the Court has had difficulty with this because the amendment is ambiguous. Over time the Supreme Court has concluded that the amendment protects property in some circum-stances, privacy in other circumstances, and neither property nor privacy in other circumstances. Deciding when property or privacy interests are impor-tant enough to be protected has not been easy.

While the Fourth Amendment appears on the surface to be a simple statement of when and where government may "search and seize," it turns out to be anything but simple. First, the amendment does not outlaw *all* searches and seizures, only "unreasonable" searches and seizures, and it does not provide any real guidelines as to what is unreasonable. Second, the amendment states "The right of the people to be secure in their persons, houses, papers, and effects, against unreasonable searches and seizures, shall not be violated." Is the list "persons, houses, papers, and effects" intended to be exhaustive of the items covered by the amendment or simply to convey an idea of the kinds of things that are to be protected? Third, the amendment states that warrants shall only be issued if they are supported by "probable cause." What does "probable cause" mean? Fourth, does the amendment mean that searches and seizures may only take place if a warrant is first obtained, or does it simply mean that if a warrant is obtained, because a warrant is needed in a particular situation, then the warrant must fulfill the requirements spelled out in the amendment? The Supreme Court did not begin to answer these questions until almost a century after the Fourth Amendment had been added to the Constitution.

THE FIRST SEARCH AND SEIZURE CASE

The year was 1886, and the case, *Boyd v. United States*, involved glass merchants charged with possessing 35 cases of imported plate glass upon which the proper customs duties had not been paid. The main issue of the case was whether or not the merchants had purchased the glass from a domestic supplier or from smugglers, so a judge ordered the defendants to bring an invoice for the glass into Court. The merchants refused, arguing that this amounted to an unreasonable search and seizure in violation of the Fourth Amendment.

With an opinion written by Justice Bradley, a unanimous Supreme Court agreed with the merchants that they did not have to produce the invoice as ordered by the judge. The Court refused to limit the scope of the Fourth Amendment to its exact words. While no government official had actually entered the merchant's place of business to search and seize the invoice, the Court thought that ordering the merchants to produce the item amounted to the same thing and violated the Fourth Amendment. Nor did the justices discuss whether or not an invoice for plate glass was really what the authors of the Fourth Amendment had in mind when they wrote that "papers and effects" should be protected from unreasonable searches and seizures.

Justice Bradley spoke in expansive terms about the scope of the amendment, arguing that it should "apply to all invasions on the part of the government and its employees of the sanctity of a man's home and the privacies of life." Of course, in *Boyd* the government and its employees had not entered anyone's home or in any real sense invaded anyone's privacy. Justice Bradley went on to say that "it is not the breaking of his doors, and the rummaging of his drawers, that constitutes the essence of the offense; but it is the invasion of his indefeasible right of personal security, personal liberty and private property" that the Fourth Amendment was intended to prevent. In Justice Bradley's view, the amendment was intended to protect the "privacies of life" from the "arbitrary power" of "petty officers." The fact that in this case the "petty officer" was a judge and the "arbitrary power" was a court order asking for the production of documents did not matter to the Supreme Court in 1886. In the opinion of all the justices, the essence, the fundamental purpose of the amendment had been violated by this government action.

This first case set the Court on a course of Fourth Amendment interpretation that would be far from what anyone could call strict construction, if by strict construction we mean interpreting a provision to mean only what it literally says. The words of the amendment would be seen as an expression of a general goal to be achieved rather than a set of specific instructions. Just as the First Amendment's command that "Congress shall make no law respecting an establishment of religion" has been interpreted to mean that no government or legislature may support religion, so the Fourth Amendment's command to protect "persons, houses, papers, and effects" would come to protect the "privacies of life." Protecting privacy from arbitrary invasion by government was seen to be a fundamental goal by the Court in this first case.

When it comes to the amendments that make up the Bill of Rights, the Supreme Court has found it almost impossible to even begin interpreting them without first deciding what the main goals of the amendments are. In 1886 the Court expressed the view that the Fourth Amendment was designed to protect both property rights and the right to keep some things private. Over the years, the Court sometimes emphasized either property or privacy in its interpretations of the Fourth Amendment but always came back to the conclusion that both were intended to be protected.

In *Boyd* the Court also pointed out that the evil uppermost in the minds of the members of Congress who voted to place the Fourth Amendment into the Constitution was the uncontrolled power of government officials. In 1761 James Otis had complained that customs officials had total discretion to decide who they would and would not search, which allowed them to harass their personal enemies while leaving their friends alone. In 1886 in this first decision, the Court made the point that there must be some limits on this kind of discretion when fundamental rights, such as the right to be secure in a home or business, are concerned.

CREATING THE EXCLUSIONARY RULE

The next major decision by the Court in this area was again unanimous, but it came almost three decades later, in 1914, with *Weeks v. United States*. Fremont Weeks was arrested as he stepped from a train at Union Station in Kansas City and charged with selling lottery tickets by mail. While one policeman was arresting him at the station, another was going through his house in search of evidence without a search warrant. The question before the Court was whether or not the evidence obtained by this search could be used at Fremont Weeks's trial.

A unanimous Court ruled that the evidence taken from Weeks's house would have to be excluded from any trial because it had been obtained in violation of the Fourth Amendment, and that Fremont Weeks's conviction had to be overturned. Justice Day, who wrote the opinion for the Court, said, as Justice Bradley had said before, that the Fourth Amendment was intended to protect Americans from "invasions of the home and privacy" and to protect their "private papers," which had been taken in this case to use as evidence. Quoting legal scholars, Justice Day argued that the purpose of the Fourth Amendment was to insure that "every man's house is his castle" and that the "privacies of life" should be protected. It did not matter that the "privacies of life" in this case consisted of business documents and stock certificates. He continued:

> If letters and private documents can thus be seized and held and used in evidence against a citizen accused of an offense, the protection of the Fourth Amendment declaring his right to be secure against such searches and seizures is of no value, and, so far as those thus placed are concerned, might as well be stricken from the Constitution. The efforts of the courts and their officials to bring the guilty to punishment, praiseworthy as they are, are not to be aided by the sacrifice of those great principles established by years of endeavor and suffering which have resulted in their embodiment in the fundamental law of the land.

With this decision in *Weeks* the Court had begun to create the exclusionary rule. The rule would say that, in some cases, things seized in violation of the Fourth Amendment may not be used as evidence in court.

TRESPASS AND THE FOURTH AMENDMENT

While in *Weeks* the Court ruled that government officials had no right to search a man's home without a search warrant, that ruling was not based on the law of trespass. This is one of the fundamental misunderstandings many people have about the scope of the Fourth Amendment—they assume that the amendment was intended to protect people from government trespass on private property. The Supreme Court has never tied the Fourth Amendment to the law of trespass.

This is illustrated by the Court's unanimous decision in the 1924 case of *Hester v. United States*, with an opinion by Justice Holmes. Two federal revenue agents waited in the bushes 100 yards from Charlie Hester's home (on Charlie Hester's farm) to see whether he was selling moonshine whiskey. When the agents saw a jug being exchanged for money, they jumped out of the bushes, chased both Hester and his customer, and caught them. Charlie Hester's attorney argued that since the two agents had been hiding on private property they had violated Hester's right to be free from police trespass protected by the Fourth Amendment. If the Fourth Amendment was simply a rule against trespass by government agents on private real estate, that argument would have ended the case, but a unanimous Court ruled that such was not the function of the Fourth Amendment. While the amendment protected "persons, houses, papers, and effects," it did not protect "open fields." Since the Fourth Amendment had not been violated in this case, the evidence did not need to be excluded and Charlie Hester's conviction was affirmed.

If the amendment protects more than just "persons, houses, papers, and effects," (businesses, for example), but it does not protect a farmer from trespass by government agents on his private property if that private property is merely an "open field," then what exactly does the amendment protect? The Court began to answer that question in the next major search and seizure case.

WIRETAPPING AND THE *OLMSTEAD* CASE

With the 1928 case of *Olmstead v. United States* (see p. 21), the Court divided five to four. Roy Olmstead had been convicted of a conspiracy to violate the National Prohibition Act by unlawfully possessing, transporting, importing, and selling intoxicating liquors. In order to find out what Olmstead was doing and who he was working with, federal agents used a series of wiretaps on his and other people's telephones, placing taps on the wires outside the suspects' homes and offices. In other words, in this case there was no trespass on private property.

Chief Justice Taft, writing for the five-justice majority, stated:

> [T]he well known historical purpose of the Fourth Amendment, directed against general warrants and writs of assistance, was to prevent the use of governmental force to search a man's house, his person, his papers and his effects; and to prevent their seizure against his will.

He went on to say:

> The Amendment does not forbid what was done here. There was no searching. There was no seizure. The evidence was secured by the use of the sense of hearing and that only. There was no entry of the houses or offices of the defendants.

Chief Justice Taft believed that outlawing wiretaps would expand the Fourth Amendment "beyond the practical meaning of houses, persons, papers and effects." Because the information obtained through the use of the wiretaps did not have to be excluded, Olmstead's conviction was affirmed.

Justices Holmes, Brandeis, Butler, and Stone dissented. Justice Brandeis, writing what would become one of the most famous dissenting opinions in Supreme Court history, argued that the Court had never tied the Fourth Amendment either to the law of trespass or to the specific list of "persons, houses, papers, and effects." Rather, from the 1886 decision in *Boyd* to this decision in 1928, the Court had considered the "privacies of life" to be protected by the Fourth Amendment. Justice Brandeis pointed out:

> Whenever a telephone line is tapped, the privacy of the persons at both ends of the line is invaded and all conversations between them upon any subject, and although proper, confidential and privileged may be over-heard. Moreover, the tapping of one man's telephone line involves the tapping of the telephone of every other person whom he may call or who may call him. As a means of espionage, writs of assistance and general warrants are but puny instruments of tyranny and oppression when compared with wire-tapping. . . . The protection guaranteed by the Amendments is much broader in scope. The makers of our Constitution undertook to secure conditions favorable to the pursuit of happiness. They recognized the significance of man's spiritual nature, of his feelings and of his intellect. They knew that only a part of the pain, pleasure and satisfactions of life are to be found in material things. They sought to protect Americans in their beliefs, their thoughts, their emotions and their sensations. They conferred, as against the Government, the right to be let alone—the most comprehensive of rights and the right most valued by civilized men. To protect that right, every unjustifiable intrusion by the Government upon the privacy of the individual, whatever the means employed, must be deemed a violation of the Fourth Amendment.

This may well be the most quoted passage ever penned by a Supreme Court justice. Justice Brandeis had finally stated explicitly what had been implicit in previous decisions, that the Fourth Amendment protects the right of privacy, the right to be left alone, free from unreasonable government interference. In his opinion, the purpose of the Fourth Amendment, and the Bill of Rights in general, was to place a wall between government and the people. There would be a private sphere and a sphere that government would be free to invade, and it would be up to the Court to draw the line between these two spheres. In Justice Brandeis's opinion, since the police would have had to trespass and invade privacy to listen to a private conversation in a private home, doing the same thing by electronic means should also qualify as a violation of the Fourth Amendment.

Justice Butler also wrote a dissenting opinion in which he said:

> This Court has always construed the Constitution in the light of the principles upon which it was founded. The direct operation or literal meaning of the words used do not measure the purpose or scope of its provisions. Under the principles established and applied by this Court, the Fourth Amendment safeguards against all evils that are like and equivalent to those embraced within the ordinary meaning of its words.

For Justice Butler the evil was, put simply, government snooping into people's private lives, and that could take many forms. The fact that new inventions, such as the telephone, allowed snooping to assume new forms, only meant that the Court must act to protect privacy in the face of new technology.

THE REASONABLE EXPECTATION OF PRIVACY

Finally, in the 1967 case of *Katz v. United States* (see p. 24), the *Olmstead* decision was overturned. Charles Katz had been convicted of transmitting wagering information by telephone from Los Angeles to Miami and Boston, which was a federal crime. The evidence was acquired by bugging a public telephone booth often used by Charles Katz.

Writing for the eight-justice majority, Justice Stewart said that the Fourth Amendment protects both "property" and "privacy," and the justices who decided the *Olmstead* case were wrong to emphasize only the property interests. The majority in *Katz* formerly overruled the *Olmstead* decision. Justice Stewart went on to say:

> The Government's activities in electronically listening to and recording the petitioner's words violated the privacy upon which he justifiably relied while using the telephone booth and thus constituted a "search and seizure" within the meaning of the Fourth Amendment.

Justice Harlan wrote a concurring opinion, in which he summarized what he believed to be the main point of the case. Because of his brief and concise language, it is often Justice Harlan's statement that is quoted concerning the meaning of the *Katz* decision. Justice Harlan said:

> I join the opinion of the Court, which I read to hold only (a) that an enclosed telephone booth is an area where, like a home, *Weeks v. United States*, 232 U.S. 383, and unlike a field, *Hester v. United States*, 265 U.S. 57, a person has a constitutionally protected reasonable expectation of privacy; (b) that electronic as well as physical intrusion into a place that is in this sense private may constitute a violation of the Fourth Amendment; and (c) that the invasion of a constitutionally protected area by federal authorities is, as the Court has long held, presumptively unreasonable in the absence of a search warrant.

Justice Harlan continued:

> My understanding of the rule that has emerged from prior decisions is that there is a twofold requirement, first that a person have exhibited an actual (subjective) expectation of privacy and, second, that the expectation be one that society is prepared to recognize as "reasonable."

The phrase most often taken from this opinion is the "reasonable expectation of privacy." The Fourth Amendment protects people who have "an . . . expectation of privacy" in situations and places where it is "reasonable" for them to have such an expectation. The amendment does not protect open fields, because it would not be reasonable for people to expect to be unobserved in an open field. Telephone conversations are protected, because people may reasonably expect that what they say over the telephone will not be overheard by anyone other than the parties to the conversation. People are reasonable to expect privacy in their homes. They are not reasonable to expect privacy when they walk out on the public street or throw open their windows for everyone to hear or see what is going on inside.

Over the next 25 years, both Supreme Court justices and commentators would refer back to Justice Harlan's concept of the "reasonable expectation of privacy." Too often lost in the discussion would be the fact that Justice Stewart had written the majority opinion, not Justice Harlan, and Justice Stewart had pointed out, correctly, that the Supreme Court had never tied the Fourth Amendment to just privacy or just property but to a combination of the two concepts. In some situations the amendment would protect privacy without private property, such as a telephone booth, while in other situations it would protect private property without privacy, such as the area around a private home.

Justice Black, the only dissenting justice in this case, argued for a stricter interpretation of the Fourth Amendment:

> My basic objection is twofold: (1) I do not believe that the words of the Amendment will bear the meaning given them by today's decision, and (2) I do not believe that it is the proper role of this Court to rewrite the Amendment in order "to bring it into harmony with the times" and thus reach a result that many people believe to be desirable.

The words "persons, houses, papers, and effects," Justice Black believed, can only be stretched so far and no farther. "These words connote the idea of tangible things with size, form, and weight, things capable of being searched, seized, or both." Because a phone conversation over an electric wire does not have size and form, in his opinion it could not be protected by the Fourth Amendment. His arguments were almost a century too late. There was no search and seizure in the usual sense of those words in the 1886 *Boyd* case, yet a unanimous Supreme Court found the order to bring an invoice to Court to be "unreasonable" and a violation of the Fourth Amendment. There had been an unreasonable intrusion into what the Court considered to be the private sphere by governmental officials.

CONCLUSION

While some people have debated the question of whether or not the Fourth Amendment can be subjected to what we might call strict construction, with the exception of Justice Black the members of the Court have not spilled much ink on this question. They have recognized from the beginning that the vague language of the Fourth Amendment granted to the members of the Supreme Court the power to determine what it did and did not protect. The use of phrases such as "unreasonable" and "probable cause" would clearly require a great deal of analysis and explanation by the justices of the Supreme Court. For example, surely the members of the first Congress must have had James Otis in mind when they wrote the Fourth Amendment even though they left the word "business" out of the list of things protected. Just as clearly in the minds of most justices, the first Congress could not have intended a warrant to be used in every case, because that would make law enforcement all but impossible. What about emergencies? What about special circumstances where the time required to obtain a warrant would defeat the purpose of the warrant because the evidence would be moved or destroyed?

The Court did take the position throughout the first half of the twentieth century that in most situations the Fourth Amendment required officials to obtain a warrant before a search or seizure unless there were special circumstances that justified not doing so. Over time, however, the list of "special circumstances" would become so long that some justices would wish the Court had taken a different approach. By then it would be too late.

In the minds of most justices, the Fourth Amendment should protect both property and privacy and should act to insulate people from the uncontrolled power of government officials. At the same time, the amendment should not unreasonably interfere with law enforcement. Striking a balance between these two goals would prove to be difficult.

CASE DECISIONS

Olmstead v. United States held that the Fourth Amendment did not prohibit wiretapping by government officials and that wiretapping could be done without the need for either a warrant or probable cause. Chief Justice Taft wrote the opinion for the majority, which is included here. Justices Holmes, Brandeis, Butler, and Stone each wrote dissenting opinions. Justice Brandeis's dissenting opinion is included here. This may be the most frequently quoted dissenting opinion ever written by a Supreme Court justice.

Katz v. United States overruled the *Olmstead* decision and held that in most cases a search warrant would be required before wiretapping and bugging by government officials could take place. Justice Stewart wrote the opinion for the majority, which is included here. Justices Douglas, Harlan, and White wrote concurring opinions. Justice Harlan's concurring opinion is included here. Justice Black wrote a dissenting opinion, which is also included here.

Following are excerpts from the case decisions.

❋ ❋ ❋ ❋ ❋ ❋ ❋ ❋ ❋

OLMSTEAD v. UNITED STATES
277 U.S. 438 (1928)

MR. CHIEF JUSTICE TAFT delivered the opinion of the Court.

These cases are here by certiorari from the Circuit Court of Appeals for the Ninth Circuit. 19 F. (2d) 842 and 850. The petition in No. 493 was filed August 30, 1927; in Nos. 532 and 533, September 9, 1927. They were granted with the distinct limitation that the hearing should be confined to the single question whether the use of evidence of private telephone conversations between the defendants and others, intercepted by means of wire tapping, amounted to a violation of the Fourth and Fifth Amendments.

The petitioners were convicted in the District Court for the Western District of Washington of a conspiracy to violate the National Prohibition Act by unlawfully possessing, transporting and importing intoxicating liquors and maintaining nuisances, and by selling intoxicating liquors. Seventy-two others in addition to the petitioners were indicted. Some were not apprehended, some were acquitted and others pleaded guilty.

The evidence in the records discloses a conspiracy of amazing magnitude to import, possess and sell liquor unlawfully. It involved the employment of not less than fifty persons, of two seagoing vessels for the transportation of liquor to British Columbia, of smaller vessels for coastwise transportation to the State of Washington, the purchase and use of a ranch beyond the suburban limits of Seattle, with a large underground cache for storage and a number of smaller caches in that city, the maintenance of a central office manned with operators, the employment of executives, salesmen, deliverymen, dispatchers, scouts, bookkeepers, collectors and an attorney. In a bad month sales amounted to $176,000; the aggregate for a year must have exceeded two millions of dollars. . . .

The information which led to the discovery of the conspiracy and its nature and extent was largely obtained by intercepting messages on the telephones of the conspirators by four federal prohibition officers. Small wires were inserted along the ordinary telephone wires from the residences of four of the petitioners and those leading from the chief office. The insertions were made without trespass upon any property of the defendants. They were made in the basement of the large office building. The taps from house lines were made in the streets near the houses.

The gathering of evidence continued for many months. Conversations of the conspirators of which refreshing stenographic notes were currently made, were testified to by the government witnesses. They revealed the large business transactions of the partners and their subordinates. Men at the wires heard the orders given for liquor by customers and the acceptances; they became auditors of the conversations between the partners. All this disclosed the conspiracy charged in the indictment. Many of the intercepted conversations were not merely reports but parts of the criminal acts. The evidence also disclosed the difficulties to which the conspirators were subjected, the reported news of the capture of vessels, the arrest of their men and the seizure of cases of liquor in garages and other places. It showed the dealing by Olmstead, the chief conspirator, with members of the Seattle police, the messages to them which secured the release of arrested members of the conspiracy, and also direct promises to officers of payments as soon as opportunity offered. . . .

The [Fourth] Amendment does not forbid what was done here. There was no searching. There was no seizure. The evidence was secured by the use of the sense of hearing and that only. There was no entry of the houses or offices of the defendants.

By the invention of the telephone, fifty years ago, and its application for the purpose of extending communications, one can talk with another at a far distant place. The language of the Amendment can not be extended and expanded to include telephone wires reaching to the whole world from the defendant's house or office. The intervening wires are not part of his house or office any more than are the highways along which they are stretched. . . .

Justice Bradley in the *Boyd* case, and Justice Clark in the *Gouled* case, said that the Fifth Amendment and the Fourth Amendment were to be liberally construed to effect the purpose of the framers of the Constitution in the interest of liberty. But that can not justify enlargement of the language employed beyond the possible practical meaning of houses, persons, papers, and effects, or so to apply the words search and seizure as to forbid hearing or sight. . . .

Neither the cases we have cited nor any of the many federal decisions brought to our attention hold the Fourth Amendment to have been violated as against a defendant unless there has been an official search and seizure of his person, or such a seizure of his papers or his tangible material effects, or an actual physical invasion of his house "or curtilage" for the purpose of making a seizure.

We think, therefore, that the wire tapping here disclosed did not amount to a search and seizure within the meaning of the Fourth Amendment.

Dissenting Opinion   MR. JUSTICE BRANDEIS, dissenting.

The Government makes no attempt to defend the methods employed by its officers. Indeed, it concedes that if wire-tapping can be deemed a search and seizure within the Fourth Amendment, such wire-tapping as was practiced in the case at bar was an unreasonable search and seizure, and that the evidence thus obtained was inadmissible. But it relies on the language of the Amendment; and it claims that the protection given thereby cannot properly be held to include a telephone conversation.

"We must never forget," said Mr. Chief Justice Marshall in *McCulloch v. Maryland*, 4 Wheat. 316, 407, "that it is a constitution we are expounding." Since then, this Court has repeatedly sustained the exercise of power by Congress, under various clauses of that instrument, over objects of which the Fathers could not have dreamed. See *Pensacola Telegraph Co. v. Western Union Telegraph Co.*, 90 U.S. 1, 9; *Northern Pacific Ry. Co. v. North Dakota*, 250 U.S. 135; *Dakota Central Telephone Co. v. South Dakota*, 250 U.S. 163; *Brooks v. United States*, 267 U.S. 432. We have likewise held that general limitations on the powers of Government, like those embodied in the due process clauses of the Fifth and Fourteenth Amendments, do not forbid the United States or the States from meeting modern conditions by regulations which "a century ago, or even half a century ago, probably would have been rejected as arbitrary and oppressive." *Village of Euclid v. Ambler Realty Co.*, 272 U.S. 365, 387; *Buck v. Bell*, 274 U.S. 200. Clauses guaranteeing to the individual protection against specific abuses of power, must have a similar capacity of adaptation to a changing world. It was with reference to such a clause that this Court said in *Weems v. United States*, 217 U.S. 349, 373: "Legislation, both statutory and constitutional, is enacted, it is true, from an experience of evils, but its general language should not, therefore, be necessarily confined to the form that evil had theretofore taken. Time works changes, brings into existence new conditions and purposes. Therefore a principle to be vital must be capable of wider application than the mischief which gave it birth. This is peculiarly true of constitutions. They are not ephemeral enactments, designed to meet passing occasions. They are, to use the words of Chief Justice Marshall 'designed to approach immortality as nearly as human institutions can approach it.' The future is their care and provision for events of good and bad tendencies of which no prophecy can be made. In the application of a constitution, therefore, our contemplation cannot be only of what has been but of what may be. Under any other rule a constitution would indeed be as easy of application as it would be deficient in efficacy and power. Its general principles would have little value and be converted by precedent into impotent and lifeless formulas. Rights declared in words might be lost in reality." . . .

The protection guaranteed by the Amendments is much broader in scope. The makers of our Constitution undertook to secure conditions favorable to the pursuit of happiness. They recognized the significance of man's spiritual nature, of his feelings and of his intellect. They knew that only a part of the pain, pleasure and satisfactions of life are to be found in material things. They sought to protect Americans in their beliefs, their thoughts, their emotions and their sensations. They conferred, as against the Government, the right to be let alone—the most comprehensive of rights and the right most valued by civilized men. To protect that right, every unjustifiable intrusion by the Government upon the privacy of the individual, whatever the means employed, must be deemed a violation of the Fourth Amendment.

KATZ v. UNITED STATES
389 U.S. 347 (1967)

MR. JUSTICE STEWART delivered the opinion of the Court.

The petitioner was convicted in the District Court for the Southern District of California under an eight-count indictment charging him with transmitting wagering information by telephone from Los Angeles to Miami and Boston, in violation of a federal statute. At trial the Government was permitted, over the petitioner's objection, to introduce evidence of the petitioner's end of telephone conversations, overheard by FBI agents who had attached an electronic listening and recording device to the outside of the public telephone booth from which he had placed his calls. In affirming his conviction, the Court of Appeals rejected the contention that the recordings had been obtained in violation of the Fourth Amendment, because "[t]here was no physical entrance into the area occupied by [the petitioner]." We granted certiorari in order to consider the constitutional questions thus presented.

The petitioner has phrased those questions as follows:

"A. Whether a public telephone booth is a constitutionally protected area so that evidence obtained by attaching an electronic listening recording device to the top of such a booth is obtained in violation of the right to privacy of the user of the booth.

"B. Whether physical penetration of a constitutionally protected area is necessary before a search and seizure can be said to be violative of the Fourth Amendment to the United States Constitution."

We decline to adopt this formulation of the issues. In the first place, the correct solution of Fourth Amendment problems is not necessarily promoted by incantation of the phrase "constitutionally protected area." Secondly, the Fourth Amendment cannot be translated into a general constitutional "right to privacy." That Amendment protects individual privacy against certain kinds of governmental intrusion, but its protections go further, and often have nothing to do with privacy at all. Other provisions of the Constitution protect personal privacy from other forms of governmental invasion. But the protection of a person's *general* right to privacy—his right to be let alone by other people—is, like the protection of his property and of his very life, left largely to the law of the individual States.

Because of the misleading way the issues have been formulated, the parties have attached great significance to the characterization of the telephone booth from which the petitioner placed his calls. The petitioner has strenuously argued that the booth was a "constitutionally protected area." The Government has maintained with equal vigor that it was not. But this effort to decide whether or not a given "area," viewed in the abstract, is "constitutionally protected" deflects attention from the problem presented by this case. For the Fourth Amendment protects people, not places. What a person knowingly exposes to the public, even in his own home or office, is not a subject of Fourth Amendment protection. See *Lewis v. United States,* 385 U.S. 206, 210; *United States v. Lee,* 274 U.S. 559, 563. But what he seeks to preserve as private, even in an area accessible to the public, may be constitutionally protected. . . .

The Government stresses the fact that the telephone booth from which the petitioner made his calls was constructed partly of glass, so that he was as visible after he entered it as he would have been if he had remained outside. But what he sought to exclude when he entered the booth was not the intruding eye—it was the uninvited ear. He did not shed his right to do so simply because he made his calls from a place where he might be seen. No less than an individual in a business office, in a friend's apartment, or in a taxicab, a person in a telephone booth may rely upon the protection of the Fourth Amendment. One who occupies it, shuts the door behind him, and pays the toll that permits him to place a call is surely entitled to assume that the words he utters into the mouthpiece will not be broadcast to the world. To read the Constitution more narrowly is to ignore the vital role that the public telephone has come to play in private communication.

The Government contends, however, that the activities of its agents in this case should not be tested by Fourth Amendment requirements, for the surveillance technique they employed involved no physical penetration of the telephone booth from which the petitioner placed his calls. It is true that the absence of such penetration was at one time thought to foreclose further Fourth Amendment inquiry, *Olmstead v. United States*, 277 U.S. 438, 457, 464, 466; *Goldman v. United States*, 316 U.S. 129, 134–136, for that Amendment was thought to limit only searches and seizures of tangible property. But "[t]he premise that property interests control the right of the Government to search and seize has been discredited." *Warden v. Hayden*, 387 U.S. 294, 304. Thus, although a closely divided Court supposed in *Olmstead* that surveillance without any trespass and without the seizure of any material object fell outside the ambit of the Constitution, we have since departed from the narrow view on which that decision rested. Indeed, we have expressly held that the Fourth Amendment governs not only the seizure of tangible items, but extends as well to the recording of oral statements, overheard without any "technical trespass under . . . local property law." *Silverman v. United States*, 365 U.S. 505, 511. Once this much is acknowledged, and once it is recognized that the Fourth Amendment protects people—and not simply "areas"—against unreasonable searches and seizures, it becomes clear that the reach of that Amendment cannot turn upon the presence or absence of a physical intrusion into any given enclosure.

We conclude that the underpinnings of *Olmstead* and *Goldman* have been so eroded by our subsequent decisions that the "trespass" doctrine there enunciated can no longer be regarded as controlling. The Government's activities in electronically listening to and recording the petitioner's words violated the privacy upon which he justifiably relied while using the telephone booth and thus constituted a "search and seizure" within the meaning of the Fourth Amendment. The fact that the electronic device employed to achieve that end did not happen to penetrate the wall of the booth can have no constitutional significance.

The question remaining for decision, then, is whether the search and seizure conducted in this case complied with constitutional standards. In that regard, the Government's position is that its agents acted in an entirely defensible manner: They did not begin their electronic surveillance until investigation of the petitioner's activities had established a strong probability that he was using the telephone in question to transmit gambling information to persons in other States, in violation of federal law. Moreover, the surveillance was limited, both in scope and in duration, to the specific purpose of establishing the contents of the petitioner's unlawful telephonic communications. The agents confined their surveillance to the brief periods during which he used the telephone booth, and they took great care to overhear only the conversations of the petitioner himself.

Accepting this account of the Government's actions as accurate, it is clear that this surveillance was so narrowly circumscribed that a duly authorized magistrate, properly notified of the need for such investigation, specifically informed of the basis on which it was to proceed, and clearly apprised of the precise intrusion it would entail, could constitutionally have authorized, with appropriate safeguards, the very limited search and seizure that the Government asserts in fact took place. Only last Term we sustained the validity of such an authorization, holding that, under sufficiently "precise and discriminate circumstances," a federal court may empower government agents to employ a concealed electronic device "for the narrow and particularized purpose of ascertaining the truth of the . . . allegations" of a "detailed factual affidavit alleging the commission of a specific criminal offense." *Osborn v. United States*, 385 U.S. 323, 329–330. Discussing that holding, the Court in *Berger v. New York*, 388 U.S. 41, said that "the order authorizing the use of the electronic device" in *Osborn* "afforded similar protections to those . . . of conventional warrants authorizing the seizure of tangible evidence." Through those protections, "no greater invasion of privacy was permitted than was necessary under the circumstances." *Id.*, at 57. Here, too, a similar judicial order could have accommodated "the legitimate needs of law enforcement" by authorizing the carefully limited use of electronic surveillance. . . .

Wherever a man may be, he is entitled to know that he will remain free from unreasonable searches and seizures. The government agents here ignored "the procedure of antecedent justification . . . that is central to the Fourth Amendment," a procedure that we hold to be a constitutional precondition of the kind of electronic surveillance involved in this case. Because the surveillance here failed to meet that condition, and because it led to the petitioner's conviction, the judgment must be reversed.

It is so ordered.

Concurring Opinion Mr. Justice Harlan, concurring.

I join the opinion of the Court, which I read to hold only (a) that an enclosed telephone booth is an area where, like a home, *Weeks v. United States*, 232 U.S. 383, and unlike a field, *Hester v. United States*, 265 U.S. 57, a person has a constitutionally protected reasonable expectation of privacy; (b) that electronic as well as physical intrusion into a place that is in this sense private may constitute a violation of the Fourth Amendment; and (c) that the invasion of a constitutionally protected area by federal authorities is, as the Court has long held, presumptively unreasonable in the absence of a search warrant.

As the Court's opinion states, "the Fourth Amendment protects people, not places." The question, however, is what protection it affords to those people. Generally, as here, the answer to that question requires reference to a "place." My understanding of the rule that has emerged from prior decisions is that there is a twofold requirement, first that a person have exhibited an actual (subjective) expectation of privacy and, second, that the expectation be one that society is prepared to recognize as "reasonable." Thus a man's home is, for most purposes, a place where he expects privacy, but objects, activities, or statements that he exposes to the "plain view" of outsiders are not "protected" because no intention to keep them to himself has been exhibited. On the other hand, conversations in the open would not be protected against being overheard, for the expectation of privacy under the circumstances would be unreasonable. Cf. *Hester v. United States, supra.*

The critical fact in this case is that "[o]ne who occupies it, [a telephone booth] shuts the door behind him, and pays the toll that permits him to place a call is surely entitled to assume" that his conversation is not being intercepted. *Ante*, at 352. The point is not that the booth is "accessible to the public" at other times, *ante*, at 351, but that it is a temporarily private place whose momentary occupants' expectations of freedom from intrusion are recognized as reasonable. Cf. *Rios v. United States*, 364 U.S. 253.

Dissenting Opinion   MR. JUSTICE BLACK, dissenting.

My basic objection is twofold: (1) I do not believe that the words of the Amendment will bear the meaning given them by today's decision, and (2) I do not believe that it is the proper role of this Court to rewrite the Amendment in order "to bring it into harmony with the times" and thus reach a result that many people believe to be desirable.

While I realize that an argument based on the meaning of words lacks the scope, and no doubt the appeal, of broad policy discussions and philosophical discourses on such nebulous subjects as privacy, for me the language of the Amendment is the crucial place to look in construing a written document such as our Constitution. The Fourth Amendment says that

> " The right of the people to be secure in their persons, houses, papers, and effects, against unreasonable searches and seizures, shall not be violated, and no Warrants shall issue, but upon probable cause, supported by Oath or affirmation, and particularly describing the place to be searched, and the persons or things to be seized."

The first clause protects "persons, houses, papers, and effects, against unreasonable searches and seizures. . . ." These words connote the idea of tangible things with size, form, and weight, things capable of being searched, seized, or both. The second clause of the Amendment still further establishes its Framers' purpose to limit its protection to tangible things by providing that no warrants shall issue but those "particularly describing the place to be searched, and the persons or things to be seized." A conversation overheard by eavesdropping, whether by plain snooping or wiretapping, is not tangible and, under the normally accepted meanings of the words, can neither be searched nor seized. In addition the language of the second clause indicates that the Amendment refers not only to something tangible so it can be seized but to something already in existence so it can be described. Yet the Court's interpretation would have the Amendment apply to overhearing future conversations which by their very nature are nonexistent until they take place. How can one "describe" a future conversation, and, if one cannot, how can a magistrate issue a warrant to eavesdrop one in the future? It is argued that information showing what is expected to be said is sufficient to limit the boundaries of what later can be admitted into evidence; but does such general information really meet the specific language of the Amendment which says "particularly describing"? Rather than using language in a completely artificial way, I must conclude that the Fourth Amendment simply does not apply to eavesdropping.

..................................DISCUSSION QUESTIONS................................

1. Upon reading the Fourth Amendment, many nonlawyers assume that its main function is to prevent trespass upon private real estate by government officials. The Supreme Court has never accepted this idea. How would the law of search and seizure be different if the Court had ruled that this was the primary function of the Fourth Amendment?

2. The Supreme Court ultimately decided that the primary function of the Fourth Amendment is to protect privacy in situations where it is reasonable for people to expect privacy. It has been up to the Court to decide which situations qualify. Do you agree with its decisions?

3. The Supreme Court finally decided, in *Katz v. United States*, that telephone conversations deserve the protection of the Fourth Amendment. Do you agree? What do you think of Justice Black's argument that phone conversations are clearly not "persons, houses, papers, and effects"?

4. The Supreme Court has said for over a century that the Fourth Amendment was intended to protect both property and privacy. Are there any other interests that you think the people who voted to place the Fourth Amendment into the Constitution might have had in mind?

5. How might you rewrite the Fourth Amendment in order to clear up some of the ambiguity?

CHAPTER
three

• • • • • • • • •

Searching Homes and Businesses

The Supreme Court has assumed that the fundamental purpose of the Fourth Amendment is to protect both property and privacy: property from search and seizure and privacy from invasion. At the same time, the Court has refused to accept arguments that the Fourth Amendment simply transferred the laws concerning trespass into the Constitution. As a general rule, the Court has found that government officials must have a warrant before trespassing on some private real estate, while other private real estate is open to invasion without either a warrant or probable cause. Drawing the line between these two types of private real estate has been a major task for the Court.

OPEN FIELDS

In the 1924 case of *Hester v. United States*, two federal revenue agents hid in the bushes on Charlie Hester's farm to witness the sale of moonshine whiskey. While this act was technically a trespass on private property, a unanimous Supreme Court did not see this as a violation of the Fourth Amendment. The agents were in an "open field," not inside a building or near the house. Over the next 50 years, as the Supreme Court modified many of its interpretations of the Fourth Amendment, scholars wondered if this "open fields" doctrine still commanded a majority on the Court.

The Supreme Court revisited this issue 60 years later in the 1984 case of *Oliver v. United States*, with Justice Powell writing the opinion for the six-justice majority. In this case Kentucky state police drove through a field on a private farm, owned by Ray Oliver, until they came to a locked gate on which there was a large "no trespassing" sign. The police then got out of their car and walked around the locked gate. Behind the locked gate, in a field well protected from public view, they found marijuana growing. Ray Oliver was convicted for growing marijuana.

Some people hoped the Court would use this case to overturn *Hester* and expand the protection of the Fourth Amendment. It did not. The justices ruled in 1984 the same way they had ruled in 1924: the Fourth Amendment does not protect private citizens from trespass by public officials on an open field. The marijuana was admissible as evidence and Ray Oliver's conviction was affirmed.

Justice Powell noted that a field is not a "person, house, paper, or effect"; therefore, it does not fall clearly within the protection of the Fourth Amendment. People do not have a legitimate expectation of privacy in an open field, he argued, even in an open field surrounded by trees, a fence, and a locked gate. While the Fourth Amendment also protects property, this is not the kind of property worthy of protection. Justice Powell reaffirmed what the Court had concluded 60 years before, that the Fourth Amendment did not simply transfer the law of trespass into the Constitution.

The three dissenting justices, Brennan, Marshall, and Stevens, argued that in this case the owner of the field had taken steps to protect the privacy of this particular field and that should make a difference. In a sense, the dissenters were arguing that this was a "closed" rather than an "open" field and therefore different rules should apply. The majority was not willing to change a rule that had been the same for six decades and that they thought struck the right balance between the privacy and property rights of the citizens and the need of law enforcement to be able to move about freely to enforce the laws.

CURTILAGE

While open fields are not protected by the Fourth Amendment, the Court has said that the *curtilage* (the area immediately around a home) is protected. But what exactly constitutes the curtilage? In the 1987 case of *United States v. Dunn*, the Court tried to shed some light on this question. The case involved federal agents who discovered that Ronald Dale Dunn had bought large quantities of chemicals. Given the kinds of chemicals he had purchased, the agents suspected him of running an illegal drug factory. They followed him to his farm and crept up to his barn where they smelled chemicals and heard a motor running. Using this information, they obtained a search warrant and returned to search the barn. Ronald Dale Dunn was subsequently convicted of manufacturing phenylacetone and amphetamine. His attorney argued that the federal agents had invaded the curtilage when they got close enough to the barn to smell the chemicals. A majority of the justices did not agree.

Justice White, writing the opinion for the Court, argued that the curtilage is the area around a home that is enclosed and evidences some desire on the part of the home owner to keep out the general public. The area these agents invaded was an open area around a barn and therefore was not part of the curtilage. Dunn's conviction would not be overturned.

Justices Brennan and Marshall dissented. Justice Brennan argued that the curtilage should include the area around both the house and the barn and any other areas that might be used for intimate behavior. While this barn was being used as a drug factory, other barns have living quarters and would certainly qualify as something more than just a barn. Because it would be impossible for police to know in advance whether the area around a particular barn would or would not qualify as "curtilage," Brennan believed the Court should simply make a general rule that the area around houses and farm buildings constitutes the curtilage. The majority of justices, however, were not willing to throw out this conviction or to define curtilage in such an expansive way.

THE VIEW FROM THE AIR

In 1986, with the case of *California v. Ciraolo*, the Court divided five to four over the issue of whether or not the Fourth Amendment had been violated. Chief Justice Burger wrote the opinion for the majority. On September 2, 1982, police in the city of Santa Clara, California, received an anonymous telephone tip that marijuana was growing in a backyard behind a high privacy fence. Police officers then got into a small plane, flew over the backyard, and saw several marijuana plants behind the privacy fence. The police used what they had seen from the air to obtain a search warrant, entered the backyard, and seized the illegal plants. The owner of the house was then convicted of marijuana cultivation.

The majority of justices believed that no one can reasonably expect privacy in his or her backyard to the extent that the backyard is subject to view from the air. Today there are planes and helicopters flying around everywhere. Anyone wishing to keep his or her backyard private should put up a tent or other device. That was not done in this case.

The Court then discussed the "curtilage" issue. In past decisions the Court had ruled that the curtilage is protected from trespass by police in the same way the inside of a home is protected. How could these decisions be reconciled with this decision? Chief Justice Burger said that while the curtilage enjoys more protection than an open field, it is not protected from being viewed from the air. It is protected from physical trespass by police unless those police are armed with a warrant. In other words, because there is no expectation of privacy from aerial view, no warrant is needed to observe the curtilage from the air. Because the curtilage is a special kind of private property (compared with open fields) police may not enter that area without a warrant. That protects the property right to the extent the Fourth Amendment protects property rights.

The four dissenting justices, Powell, Brennan, Marshall, and Blackmun, did not find this to be a reasonable distinction. In their opinion, the privacy and property interest protected by the Fourth Amendment should not be divided in this way. They argued that a backyard is protected by the Fourth Amendment because it is a curtilage and any intrusion or aerial observation should be authorized by a search warrant. The majority of justices saw this argument as simply a refusal by the dissenters to recognize the realities of modern life. Anyone can fly over a backyard, just as anyone can look at or walk across an open field, and these justices did not see why the police should be prevented from doing what anyone else can do. The conviction for marijuana possession was upheld. In the 1989 case of *Florida v. Riley*, which involved police in a helicopter, the Court came to the same conclusion.

GARBAGE

In 1988 the Court decided *California v. Greenwood*, which also concerned the reasonable expectation of privacy. Police in Laguna Beach, California, who suspected illegal activity was going on in a suburban house on a quiet residential street, asked the garbage collector to pick up the garbage at the Greenwood house and bring it straight to them instead of taking it to the dump. Their examination of the garbage revealed illegal drug activity and was used to justify a search warrant. Billy Greenwood was then convicted on drug charges.

Was the police's acquisition of the garbage a violation of the Fourth Amendment? Did this amount to an unreasonable seizure of private property? In the eyes of the majority of justices, no personal property had been seized because the owners of the garbage had turned it over to the garbage collector. If the garbage belonged to anyone at that point, it was the garbage company, not the home owner. The majority also did not think there had been an unreasonable search because there was no real invasion of privacy. In the words of Justice White, who wrote the majority opinion, "it is common knowledge that plastic garbage bags left on or at the side of a public street are readily accessible to animals, children, scavengers, snoops, and other members of the public." In other words, no one has a reasonable expectation of privacy in their garbage. If no private property has been seized and no privacy invaded, there has been no violation of the Fourth Amendment. Billy Greenwood's conviction was affirmed.

Justices Brennan and Marshall dissented, arguing that one purpose of the Fourth Amendment was to protect people from unreasonable snooping by government officials, and they believed that the police actions in this case were clearly unreasonable. The dissenting justices could envision an army of bureaucrats going through everyone's garbage to find out about their private lives, a prospect that reminded them too much of how a totalitarian state might operate.

THE HOME

What about the home itself? The Fourth Amendment does not say "home," it says "houses," but the Supreme Court has consistently ruled that a home, whatever shape it takes, is protected from unreasonable invasion by the government. That means in most cases the government must have a warrant before invading the sanctity of a home.

Justice Butler wrote the opinion for a unanimous Court in the 1925 case of *Agnello v. United States* (see p. 44). Frank Agnello had been convicted of conspiracy to sell cocaine without paying federal taxes on the drugs in his possession. While cocaine possession was illegal in most states at that time, federal law simply required that a tax be paid on the sale of cocaine. No one paid the tax because to do so would have subjected the person to prosecution under state laws for possession of an illegal drug.

Without a search warrant, police and federal agents searched the back of a grocery store where Frank Agnello lived and introduced the cocaine they found there at his trial. Because the search was conducted without a warrant, the Supreme Court threw out Agnello's conviction. Be it ever so humble, Frank Agnello's room in the back of the grocery store was his home and was entitled to the same protection from unreasonable searches that any mansion would be entitled to. The police should have gotten a warrant before entering his home.

In the 1948 case of *Trupiano v. United States*, federal agents who did not have either a search warrant or an arrest warrant searched a private barn. The barn contained illegal distilling machines, which had been used in making illegal liquor. In this case the agents had plenty of time to obtain a search warrant—there was no emergency, no fear that anyone might be placed in danger by the delay—so there was no excuse for not obtaining one.

The Court ruled five to four that this invasion of a private barn without some kind of warrant constituted a violation of the Fourth Amendment. Did it make a difference that this was a barn rather than a house? Not to the Court. The barn was a private building on private property, not open to the general public and therefore part of the private sphere government may not invade without a warrant. The government would not be allowed to use the distilling machines as evidence that the liquor laws had been violated.

The Court also ruled in 1948, with a five-to-four decision in *Johnson v. United States*, that police need a warrant before they may enter a hotel room. The fact that in this case police smelled the strong odor of burning opium coming from the hotel room did not justify invading property and privacy without first obtaining a warrant.

EXCEPTIONS TO THE WARRANT REQUIREMENT

In the 1963 case of *Ker v. California*, George Ker had been convicted of marijuana possession. After seeing known marijuana sellers interacting with George Ker on the public street, police tried to follow Ker but lost him in traffic. The police then called in Ker's license plate number, obtained his address, and went immediately to his apartment. Because in their opinion they had good reason to believe that marijuana was in Ker's house, the police entered unannounced, without a warrant, in order to keep the marijuana from being destroyed.

The five-justice majority accepted the argument that time was of the essence in this case because the marijuana could have been destroyed before the police obtained a warrant to enter the apartment. Because George Ker had been alerted to the police's interest in him by their effort to follow him, the majority did not think it would be reasonable to require the police to obtain a warrant. In the majority opinion, written by Justice Clark, the Court reaffirmed previous decisions: police do not have to obtain a warrant if the time delay would make it more difficult to obtain the evidence or arrest the person. The Court ruled that in "exigent" circumstances, meaning emergencies or other situations where time would defeat the purpose of the search, the police do not have to obtain a warrant to search a home. George Ker's conviction was affirmed.

In the 1967 case of *Warden v. Hayden*, Justice Brennan wrote an opinion from which only Justice Douglas dissented. The case involved police in "hot pursuit" of an armed robber. They followed him to a house where they found him pretending to be asleep in an upstairs bedroom. The police not only seized him, they seized the clothes that they believed he had just worn during the robbery. The robber's attorney accepted the fact that the police had a right to enter this house without a warrant because they were in hot pursuit of an armed robber, but he objected to the seizure of the clothes because they were considered under the ancient English common law to be "mere evidence." By the 1960s police and courts around the country were having great difficulty trying to live with ancient distinctions between "mere evidence," which police were not allowed to seize, and the "instrumentalities of crime," which they were allowed to seize. Are the clothes worn by a robber mere evidence or instrumentalities of crime?

Justice Brennan ruled that it was time to forget about these ancient distinctions. From 1967 on, evidence would no longer be suppressed because of these ancient rules, but rather because it had been seized in a way that violated the Fourth Amendment as interpreted by the Supreme Court. The Fourth Amendment, Justice Brennan argued, is not tied to the dictates of the ancient English common law. The amendment was instead intended to serve as the basis for the development of new U.S. law that would be separate and distinct from the ancient English rules.

Looking back on this and other decisions in the 1960s and 1970s, it is hard to believe the hold the ancient English common law rules still had on the rules of criminal procedure in the United States at such a late date. When the press decried the "confusion" caused by the law surrounding the Fourth Amendment, it failed to point out that during this period American law was in transition and was still deeply involved in breaking away from the ancient English common law rules. Much of the confusion revolved around the question of which of these ancient rules were going to survive. With the *Warden* decision in 1967, the Supreme Court went a long way toward clearing up the confusion and setting the law of search and seizure on a modern footing.

In the 1984 decision of *Michigan v. Clifford*, the Court divided five to four over when an emergency situation that justifies an invasion of property without a warrant is over. Justice Powell wrote the majority opinion. Raymond and Emma Clifford had their home burned badly in a fire. Several hours after the fire had been put out, as the house was being boarded up, arson investigators returned to the scene to investigate for arson. They found evidence of arson and Emma and Raymond Clifford were eventually convicted of burning down their own home to collect the insurance. The Supreme Court threw out the conviction. The majority of justices believed that once the fire was out the Cliffords had a reasonable expectation of privacy in their fire-damaged home. Arson investigators may investigate right after the fire is put out, the majority ruled, because they are part of the fire department team allowed to enter the property to deal with an emergency, the fire itself. If the investigators decide to come back later, however, then they need a warrant to enter the building just like any other government official.

Justice Rehnquist wrote a dissenting opinion, which was joined by Chief Justice Burger and Justices Blackmun and O'Connor. He argued that this was just another confusing decision on search and seizure. How long can the arson investigators wait for the building to cool down before beginning their investigation? What are the rules concerning when the right to enter the building without a warrant ends? How are arson investigators to know when they do and do not need a warrant in these circumstances? The majority answered that the issue was one of reasonableness, as is always the case with the Fourth Amendment, and it is not always possible to put reasonableness in such concrete terms. It is reasonable to enter a burning house because of the emergency caused by the fire and to investigate for arson while fighting the fire or just after the fire is put out. At some point, the emergency justification wears off, however, and the house again becomes subject to the usual protections of the Fourth Amendment.

During the summer of 1994, millions of Americans watched O.J. Simpson's preliminary hearing on television. A key issue was whether police were justified in entering the curtilage around O.J. Simpson's home without a search warrant. Police argued that they had good reason to believe the people in the house might be in danger and acted on that assumption. The trial judge accepted the police justification and allowed evidence discovered in the yard to be introduced at the hearing.

REGULATORY INSPECTIONS OF HOMES

If a search warrant is generally required before police may enter a home without the resident's consent, what happens if the government agents wishing to search a home are health inspectors rather than police? The 1967 case of *Camara v. Municipal Court* addressed this issue. Only Justice Clark dissented from the majority opinion, written by Justice White, which stated the Fourth Amendment protects property and privacy from invasion by government officials, even health inspectors. While the majority of justices assumed that most people would consent to having the health inspector in their home or business, those people who did not had a right to be protected from arbitrary actions by government officials. Did this mean that a health inspector must have probable cause to believe there is a health code violation before obtaining a warrant and entering private property? No, the majority of justices thought that would also be unreasonable. While police investigations are usually focused on a particular suspect and a particular home or business, health inspectors usually believe there is a problem in a block or area. Therefore, they would be allowed to obtain a warrant to search in such an area for health violations if they satisfied the judge that they had good reason to make the inspections and were not using their power in an arbitrary or discriminatory way.

The basis of this decision is that the purpose of the Fourth Amendment is to protect property and privacy against the arbitrary power of government officials, as the Court said in 1886 in the *Boyd* case. This interest applies to searches by any government official, not just police.

BUSINESSES

The Fourth Amendment states that it protects people and houses; it does not say anything about businesses. Nevertheless, the Court has assumed from the first search and seizure decision in 1886 that businesses are protected by the Fourth Amendment. In a unanimous decision in the 1921 case of *Gouled v. United States*, the Court confirmed this conclusion. Felix Gouled had been charged with conspiracy to defraud the U.S. Army. As part of the investigation, an agent from army intelligence pretended to be friendly with Felix Gouled and gained admission to his office without a warrant. When Felix Gouled was out of the room, the agent went through Gouled's private papers and found evidence of conspiracy.

The Supreme Court threw out the conviction. The Court ruled that government officials need a warrant to search through and seize private papers in a private business office. Justice Clarke, in writing the majority opinion, said that it does not make any difference whether a home or a business office is being searched; the invasion of "security and privacy" is the same.

The Court reached the same conclusion in the 1968 case of *Mancusi v. DeForte*. In this case, federal agents searched the office of Frank DeForte, vice president of a Teamsters union local, at the union headquarters without a warrant in order to seize the union's books. Justice Harlan, writing for the majority, ruled that this was a search of a private office and the agents should have obtained a warrant before conducting the search. The Fourth Amendment protects private offices, including union offices. Frank DeForte's conviction was overturned.

Three justices dissented, arguing that the papers in question did not belong to Frank DeForte and therefore he did not have standing to complain. The majority did not agree. The papers were in his private office, he had a reasonable expectation of privacy in his private office, and that privacy had been unreasonably violated by the federal government.

Regulatory Inspections of Businesses

What if the person searching a business is a government official other than the police? In the 1967 case of *See v. City of Seattle*, the Court ruled as it had in the *Camara* case—government officials must have a warrant to search a private business. In *See* a fire inspector wanted to inspect a locked commercial warehouse without a warrant. Justice White, writing for the majority, said that the purpose of the Fourth Amendment was to assure that the "decision to enter and inspect will not be the product of the unreviewed discretion of the enforcement officer in the field." Because the warehouse was not open to the general public, the owner had every right to ask to see a warrant before allowing the fire inspector inside.

Areas Open to the Public

What if the government official is in an area of a business that is open to the general public? That is different. In the 1985 case of *Maryland v. Macon*, an undercover police officer purchased an obscene magazine in an adult bookstore and then arrested the sales clerk, Baxter Macon, for selling it to him. A majority of the justices did not see any problem with this procedure. Baxter Macon's conviction was upheld. The police officer did not need a warrant to be where the general public is allowed to be. If a business opens its doors to the general public, then the police and other government officials may walk in just like everyone else. The magazines were not seized, merely purchased. Baxter Macon could not complain if the police did what the general public is allowed to do—walk into the Silver News adult bookstore in Hyattsville, Maryland, and purchase one of the products for sale.

Justices Brennan and Marshall dissented, arguing that before undercover police go into a business to purchase products, they should have to obtain a warrant in order to protect business people from the discretion of the police. Justice O'Connor, writing for the majority, did not see any reason to prevent the police from going where everyone else is allowed to go. In a sense, the part of a business that is open to the general public is like an open field on a farm. It is not an area where anyone has a reasonable expectation of privacy, and it is not an area where the property interest deserves protection.

ARREST WARRANTS

Do police need a warrant to enter a home or business to make an arrest rather than to conduct a search? If they have an arrest warrant, does it entitle them to conduct a search? In the 1947 case of *Harris v. United States*, the Court divided five to four over this question. Chief Justice Vinson wrote the opinion for the majority. FBI agents, holding arrest warrants, had entered George Harris's home looking for him. Although they did not find George Harris, they did find altered government documents, which were later used to convict Harris of illegal document alteration. The majority of justices thought that the arrest warrant justified the invasion of property and privacy in this case. The search was aimed at finding the means and instrumentalities of crime and was therefore valid. George Harris's conviction was upheld.

The four dissenting justices did not agree. They asked what had happened to the Fourth Amendment's direct command that a warrant state specifically what is to be searched for and what is to be seized. The majority of justices believed that the arrest warrant met that requirement in that it stated that it was George Harris himself the FBI agents were searching for, and anything else they happened to see while in his house should be available as evidence at his trial. The dissenting justices argued that this turned the arrest warrant into the kind of general warrant that James Otis had argued against in 1761.

The Court took up this issue again with the 1969 case of *Chimel v. California* (see p. 47). Only Justices White and Black dissented. In this case police armed with an arrest warrant went to Ted Chimel's house to wait for him. When he arrived they arrested him and then conducted a complete search of his home in Santa Ana, California.

The issue that the Court had to face squarely was whether an arrest warrant can justify a complete search of a home where an arrest takes place. The majority of justices thought that this violated the Fourth Amendment's command that the warrant state what is to be searched for and seized. An arrest warrant authorizes the police to enter the home of the person sought and to search for him or her. That means the police may look in a closet where a person might hide but not in a drawer. Once the police have the person in custody, they may search the person and the area immediately around him or her for weapons and evidence. The justification for this brief search is to protect the safety of the arresting officers. They may not conduct a full search of the home, however, without a search warrant.

In reviewing past decisions by the Court, Justice Stewart, who wrote the majority opinion, found them to be anything but consistent. Even decisions by the same group of past justices were contradictory. Some decisions seemed to suggest that an arrest warrant served as a general license to search the entire area where a person is arrested, while others seemed to limit the power to search during an arrest to only the body of the person arrested. In Justice Stewart's opinion, allowing the police to look for people in their own homes and to search them and the area in their immediate control, satisfied the legitimate needs of law enforcement. If police wished to conduct a complete search of a person's home at the same time, they could easily obtain a search warrant when they obtained the arrest warrant, and that is what they should do in most instances. Ted Chimel's conviction was overturned.

The *Chimel* decision was concerned with the extent to which an arrest warrant authorizes police to search a home. Surprisingly, the Court did not deal with the fundamental question of whether or not police need an arrest warrant to simply arrest people in their own homes until the 1980 case of *Payton v. New York*. Justice Stevens wrote the opinion for the majority. The case involved a New York statute that authorized police in New York to make felony arrests in people's homes without a warrant of any kind. Police, without a warrant, broke into Theodore Payton's apartment to arrest him. Payton was not home, but the police did find evidence that was later used to convict Payton of murder. The Supreme Court ruled that this search clearly violated the dictates of the Fourth Amendment. The key to this case was whether or not the government's interest in arresting a felon overrode the privacy interest people have in their homes. The Court ruled that it did not.

Justice Stevens pointed out that the Fourth Amendment was designed to limit the uncontrolled discretion of government officials and to protect property and privacy from the exercise of that uncontrolled discretion by requiring government officials to obtain a warrant before entering a home or business. While police do not need an arrest warrant to arrest someone on a public street, they do need one to make an arrest in a private home. It is interesting, and disturbing, that Justice Stevens discussed at length the ancient English common law rules on this subject. He concluded his discussion by stating that he found a "surprising lack of judicial decisions and a deep divergence among scholars" concerning what the ancient English common law rules required in this area.

Justice Blackmun, in his concurring opinion, did not discuss the ancient English common law rules. He noted that the Fourth Amendment required the Court to balance the needs of law enforcement against the legitimate privacy and property interests of the people. In the case of making an arrest in a home, he argued, the balance went in favor of the people. The police would have to get an arrest warrant in the absence of some emergency or special circumstance, such as hot pursuit of a fleeing felon. Theodore Payton's conviction was overturned.

Chief Justice Burger and Justices White and Rehnquist dissented, arguing that it was unreasonable to ask police to obtain arrest warrants whenever they wanted to arrest someone in a home. In their view, the balance between government and privacy interests should go the other way. Justice White wrote a long dissenting opinion in which he discussed the dictates of the ancient English common law at length. Justice Rehnquist's dissenting opinion was much shorter. He did not think a convicted murderer should be allowed to go free because of a technicality of constitutional law.

The Court discussed this issue again in the 1981 case of *Steagald v. United States*. Justice Marshall wrote the opinion for the seven-justice majority. In this case police searched Gary Steagald's home in an effort to find Ricky Lyons, for whom they had an arrest warrant. They did not find Ricky Lyons, but they did find cocaine. Did a simple arrest warrant authorize the police to enter any home or business to search for the accused? A majority of the justices of the Supreme Court did not think so, because such authority would make arrest warrants the modern equivalent of the ancient general warrants that the Boston merchants had objected to in 1761. The Court ruled that an arrest warrant for Ricky Lyons is a license to look for Ricky Lyons in his own home, but not in other people's homes or private offices. Justice Marshall wrote a long discussion of the ancient English common law rules concerning what an arrest warrant authorized in the 1700s. Justices Rehnquist and White dissented.

Justices White and Rehnquist were the only dissenters again in the 1984 case of *Welsh v. Wisconsin*. Justice Brennan wrote the opinion for the majority. In this case police, without an arrest or search warrant, arrested Edward Welsh in his home for driving under the influence of intoxicants. The police came to Edward Welsh's home after he had driven his car into a field and walked home. The majority of justices did not think this justified the police's entry into a home without a warrant. There was no hot pursuit of a felon, no emergency, and no armed and dangerous criminal, merely a possible traffic-law violator. In such circumstances, the Court ruled, the police need a warrant to enter the sanctity of a home.

On the other hand, with the 1990 case of *Maryland v. Buie*, Justices Brennan and Marshall dissented from an opinion written by Justice White. In this case the police had an arrest warrant for Jerome Buie, who was wanted for armed robbery. They went to his home, arrested him, and then walked through the house to make sure there were no other armed and dangerous individuals present. In the course of this walk through, a police officer found a red running suit, which was out in plain view. He picked it up and took it to the police station. The running suit was later used as evidence in Jerome Buie's trial because the person who committed the armed robbery in question had been wearing a red running suit.

The majority of justices agreed that the police were justified to walk through the house quickly to make sure there were no armed individuals who might jeopardize their safety when making the arrest. If they saw something in plain view, they could pick it up, just as they could pick up something lying on a public street. While the arrest warrant did not authorize a search of Buie's home, it did justify a protective walk through. Justice White ruled that such a "protective sweep" must be limited to a quick search, incident to arrest, for weapons or other criminals that might pose a danger to the police or the general public. Before making such a "protective sweep," the police must have a reasonable belief that there might be other criminals in the house who could pose a danger.

Justice White ruled that the arrest warrant was a license to look for Buie in his home. Once Buie was found, the police could make a quick sweep through the house but then had to leave. Justice White did not think this was inconsistent with the decision in *Chimel*. That case involved a full search of the house for evidence after Chimel had been taken into custody. This case involved a quick walk-through to make sure the house was safe. Jerome Buie's conviction was upheld.

CONCLUSION

When it comes to searching places, the Supreme Court has drawn a line between areas that are protected by the Fourth Amendment and areas that are not. The prime areas protected by the Fourth Amendment are homes, curtilages, and such private areas of businesses as private offices or locked warehouses. Open fields are not protected from police observation. The area of a business that is open to the public is also not protected.

Generally, before they may enter one of the private areas protected by the Fourth Amendment, police need a warrant or "exigent circumstances," such as an emergency or the belief that evidence will be destroyed in the time it takes to obtain a warrant. Arrest warrants authorize the police to search for individuals named in the warrants in their own homes, but not in anyone else's home. For that the police would need a search warrant.

CASE DECISIONS

In *Agnello v. United States*, Frank Agnello was arrested for illegal possession of cocaine. The cocaine was found in Agnello's home after a search was conducted without a warrant. A unanimous Supreme Court overturned his conviction, ruling that this search violated the Fourth Amendment. Justice Butler wrote the opinion for the Court, which is included here.

Chimel v. California concerned the question of whether or not an arrest warrant gives police the power to conduct a full search of the house of the person they are seeking to arrest. Justice Stewart wrote the opinion for the majority, which is included here, holding that an arrest warrant cannot be used to justify a full search. Justice Harlan wrote a concurring opinion and Justice White wrote a dissenting opinion, neither of which are included.

Following are excerpts from the case decisions.

❀ ❀ ❀ ❀ ❀ ❀ ❀ ❀ ❀

AGNELLO v. UNITED STATES
269 U.S. 20 (1925)

MR. JUSTICE BUTLER delivered the opinion of the Court.

Thomas Agnello, Frank Agnello, Stephen Alba, Antonio Centorino and Thomas Pace were indicted in the District Court, Eastern District of New York, under § 37, Criminal Code, c. 321, 35 Stat. 1088, 1096, for a conspiracy to violate the Harrison Act, c. 1, 38 Stat. 785, as amended by §§ 1006, 1007, 1008 of the Revenue Act of 1918, c. 18, 40 Stat. 1057, 1130. The indictment charges that defendants conspired together to sell cocaine without having registered with the Collector of Internal Revenue and without having paid the prescribed tax. The overt acts charged are that defendants had cocaine in their possession, solicited the sale of it, met in the home of defendant Alba at 138 Union Street, Brooklyn, and made arrangements for the purpose of selling it, brought a large quantity of it to that place, and sold it in violation of the Act. The jury found defendants guilty. Each was sentenced to serve two years in the penitentiary and to pay a fine of $5,000. The Circuit Court of Appeals affirmed the judgment. 290 Fed. 671.

The evidence introduced by the Government was sufficient to warrant a finding of the following facts: Pasquale Napolitano and Nunzio Dispenza, employed by government revenue agents for that purpose, went to the home of Alba, Saturday, January 14, 1922, and there offered to buy narcotics from Alba and Centorino. Alba gave them some samples. They arranged to come again on Monday following. They returned at the time agreed. Six revenue agents and a city policeman followed them and remained on watch outside. Alba left the house and returned with Centorino. They did not then produce any drug. After discussion and the refusal of Napolitano and Dispenza to go to Centorino's house to get the drug, Centorino went to fetch it. He was followed by some of the agents. He first went to his own house, 172 Columbia Street; thence to 167 Columbia Street,—one part of which was a grocery store belonging to Pace and Thomas Agnello, and another part of which, connected with the grocery store, was the home of Frank Agnello and Pace. In a short time, Centorino, Pace and the Agnellos came out of the last mentioned place, and all went to Alba's house. Looking through the windows, those on watch saw Frank Agnello produce a number of small packages for delivery to Napolitano and saw the latter hand over money to Alba. Upon the apparent consummation of the sale, the agents rushed in and arrested all the defendants. They found some of the packages on the table where the transaction took place and found others in the pockets of Frank Agnello. All contained cocaine. On searching Alba, they found the money given him by Napolitano.

And as a part of its case in chief, the Government offered testimony tending to show that, while some of the revenue agents were taking the defendants to the police station, the others and the city policeman went to the home of Centorino and searched it but did not find any narcotics; that they then went to 167 Columbia Street and searched it, and in Frank Agnello's bedroom found a can of cocaine which was produced and offered in evidence. The evidence was excluded on the ground that the search and seizure were made without a search warrant. In defense, Centorino and others gave testimony to the effect that the packages of cocaine which were brought to and seized in Alba's house at the time of the arrests had been furnished to Centorino by Dispenza to induce an apparent sale of cocaine to Napolitano, that is, to incite crime or acts having the appearance of crime, for the purpose of entrapping and punishing defendants. Centorino testified that, after leaving Napolitano and Dispenza with Alba at the latter's home, he went to his own house and got the packages of cocaine which had been given him by Dispenza and took them to 167 Columbia Street, and there gave them to Frank Agnello to be taken to Alba's house. Frank Agnello testified on direct examination that he received the packages from Centorino but that he did not know their contents, and that he would not have carried them if he had known that they contained cocaine or narcotics. On cross examination, he said that he had never seen narcotics. Then, notwithstanding objection by defendants, the prosecuting attorney produced the can of cocaine which the Government claimed was seized in Agnello's bedroom and asked him whether he had ever seen it. He said he had not, and specifically stated he had never seen it in his house. In rebuttal, over objections of defendants, the Government was permitted to put in the evidence of the search and seizure of the can of cocaine in Frank Agnello's room, which theretofore had been offered and excluded.

The case involves the questions whether search of the house of Frank Agnello and seizure of the cocaine there found, without a search warrant, violated the Fourth Amendment. . . .

The right without a search warrant contemporaneously to search persons lawfully arrested while committing crime and to search the place where the arrest is made in order to find and seize things connected with the crime as its fruits or as the means by which it was committed, as well as weapons and other things to effect an escape from custody, is not to be doubted. See *Carroll v. United States*, 267 U.S. 132, 158; *Weeks v. United States*, 232 U.S. 383, 392. The legality of the arrests or of the searches and seizures made at the home of Alba is not questioned. Such searches and seizures naturally and usually appertain to and attend such arrests. But the right does not extend to other places. Frank Agnello's house was several blocks distant from Alba's house, where the arrest was made. When it was entered and searched, the conspiracy was ended and the defendants were under arrest and in custody elsewhere. That search cannot be sustained as an incident of the arrests. / . . .

While the question has never been directly decided by this court, it has always been assumed that one's house cannot lawfully be searched without a search warrant, except as an incident to a lawful arrest therein. *Boyd v. United States*, 116 U.S. 616, 624, *et seq.*, 630; *Weeks v. United States, supra*, 393; *Silverthorne Lumber Co. v. United States, supra*, 391; *Gouled v. United States*, 255 U.S. 298, 308. The protection of the Fourth Amendment extends to all equally,—to those justly suspected or accused, as well as to the innocent. The search of a private dwelling without a warrant is in itself unreasonable and abhorrent to our laws. . . . Belief, however well founded, that an article sought is concealed in a dwelling house furnishes no justification for a search of that place without a warrant. And such searches are held unlawful notwithstanding facts unquestionably showing probable cause. . . . The search of Frank Agnello's house and seizure of the can of cocaine violated the Fourth Amendment. . . .

The admission of evidence obtained by the search and seizure was error and prejudicial to the substantial rights of Frank Agnello. The judgment against him must be set aside and a new trial awarded.

But the judgment against the other defendants may stand. The introduction of the evidence of the search and seizure did not transgress their constitutional rights. And it was not prejudicial error against them. The possession by Frank Agnello of the can of cocaine which was seized tended to show guilty knowledge and criminal intent on his part; but it was not submitted as attributable to the other defendants. During the summing up of the case to the jury by the prosecuting attorney, the court distinctly indicated that the evidence was admissible only against Frank Agnello. The other defendants did not request any instruction to the jury in reference to the matter, and they do not contend that any erroneous instruction was given. *Isaacs v. United States*, 159 U.S. 487, 491.

The packages of cocaine seized at Alba's house were carried to that place by Frank Agnello. He did this at the instance of Centorino; and in his behalf it is claimed he acted innocently and without knowledge of the contents of the package. The evidence of the search and seizure made in his house tended to show that he knew what he was doing and was a willing participant in the conspiracy charged. But so far as concerns the other defendants, it is immaterial whether he acted innocently and without knowledge of the contents of the package or knowingly to effect the object of the conspiracy. In either case, his act would be equally chargeable to his codefendants. They are not entitled to a new trial. . . .

Judgment against Frank Agnello reversed; judgment against other defendants affirmed.

CHIMEL v. CALIFORNIA
395 U.S. 752 (1969)

MR. JUSTICE STEWART delivered the opinion of the Court.

This case raises basic questions concerning the permissible scope under the Fourth Amendment of a search incident to a lawful arrest.

The relevant facts are essentially undisputed. Late in the afternoon of September 13, 1965, three police officers arrived at the Santa Ana, California, home of the petitioner with a warrant authorizing his arrest for the burglary of a coin shop. The officers knocked on the door, identified themselves to the petitioner's wife, and asked if they might come inside. She ushered them into the house, where they waited 10 or 15 minutes until the petitioner returned home from work. When the petitioner entered the house, one of the officers handed him the arrest warrant and asked for permission to "look around." The petitioner objected, but was advised that "on the basis of the lawful arrest," the officers would nonetheless conduct a search. No search warrant had been issued.

Accompanied by the petitioner's wife, the officers then looked through the entire three-bedroom house, including the attic, the garage, and a small workshop. In some rooms the search was relatively cursory. In the master bedroom and sewing room, however, the officers directed the petitioner's wife to open drawers and "to physically move contents of the drawers from side to side so that [they] might view any items that would have come from

[the] burglary." After completing the search, they seized numerous items—primarily coins, but also several medals, tokens, and a few other objects. The entire search took between 45 minutes and an hour.

At the petitioner's subsequent state trial on two charges of burglary, the items taken from his house were admitted into evidence against him, over his objection that they had been unconstitutionally seized. He was convicted, and the judgments of conviction were affirmed by both the California Court of Appeal, 61 Cal. Rptr. 714, and the California Supreme Court, 68 Cal. 2d 436, 439 P. 2d 333. Both courts accepted the petitioner's contention that the arrest warrant was invalid because the supporting affidavit was set out in conclusory terms, but held that since the arresting officers had procured the warrant "in good faith," and since in any event they had had sufficient information to constitute probable cause for the petitioner's arrest, that arrest had been lawful. From this conclusion the appellate courts went on to hold that the search of the petitioner's home had been justified, despite the absence of a search warrant, on the ground that it had been incident to a valid arrest. We granted certiorari in order to consider the petitioner's substantial constitutional claims. 393 U.S. 958.

Without deciding the question, we proceed on the hypothesis that the California courts were correct in holding that the arrest of the petitioner was valid under the Constitution. This brings us directly to the question whether the warrantless search of the petitioner's entire house can be constitutionally justified as incident to that arrest. The decisions of this Court bearing upon that question have been far from consistent, as even the most cursory review makes evident. . . .

When an arrest is made, it is reasonable for the arresting officer to search the person arrested in order to remove any weapons that the latter might seek to use in order to resist arrest or effect his escape. Otherwise, the officer's safety might well be endangered, and the arrest itself frustrated. In addition, it is entirely reasonable for the arresting officer to search for and seize any evidence on the arrestee's person in order to prevent its concealment or destruction. And the area into which an arrestee might reach in order to grab a weapon or evidentiary items must, of course, be governed by a like rule. A gun on a table or in a drawer in front of one who is arrested can be as dangerous to the arresting officer as one concealed in the clothing of the person arrested. There is ample justification, therefore, for a search of the arrestee's person and the area "within his immediate control"—construing that phrase to mean the area from within which he might gain possession of a weapon or destructible evidence.

There is no comparable justification, however, for routinely searching any room other than that in which an arrest occurs—or, for that matter, for searching through all the desk drawers or other closed or concealed areas in that room itself. Such searches, in the absence of well-recognized exceptions, may be made only under the authority of a search warrant. The "adherence to judicial processes" mandated by the Fourth Amendment requires no less. . . .

It is argued in the present case that it is "reasonable" to search a man's house when he is arrested in it. But that argument is founded on little more than a subjective view regarding the acceptability of certain sorts of police conduct, and not on considerations relevant to Fourth Amendment interests. Under such an unconfined analysis, Fourth Amendment protection in this area would approach the evaporation point. . . .

Application of sound Fourth Amendment principles to the facts of this case produces a clear result. The search here went far beyond the petitioner's person and the area from within which he might have obtained either a weapon or something that could have been used as evidence against him. There was no constitutional justification, in the absence of a search warrant, for extending the search beyond that area. The scope of the search was, therefore, "unreasonable" under the Fourth and Fourteenth Amendments, and the petitioner's conviction cannot stand.

Reversed.

·······················DISCUSSION QUESTIONS······························

1. Do you think police should have the right to trespass on an open field that has been fenced and posted with "no trespassing" signs without either a search warrant or probable cause to believe some law has been violated? The Supreme Court does. Why does the Court think it would be unreasonable to restrict police from going onto open fields with such a requirement?
2. Some justices believed the Court should distinguish between an "open field" and a "closed field." What difficulty would this kind of distinction cause for the Court?
3. The Court decided the Fourth Amendment protects a curtilage from trespass but not from being viewed from the air. Some justices argued that the Court should distinguish between police who just happen to fly over a backyard and see marijuana and police who fly over a particular

backyard in search of marijuana. If the Court had accepted this distinction, what effect do you think it might have had on the reason police would give for their flyovers?

4. Many people are bothered by the thought that police can search people's garbage without probable cause or a warrant. Given the Court's decision in this area, how would you expect people who have something to hide to behave?

5. The Court has held that police generally need a search warrant to enter the private area of a business. Can you make any good arguments that the authors of the Fourth Amendment never intended to protect businesses when they wrote the amendment?

6. An arrest warrant can not be used as a license to search everywhere for a suspect. Where can police who are armed with an arrest warrant search? If they only had an arrest warrant, would it violate the Fourth Amendment for police to break into a suspect's brother's home looking for the suspect?

CHAPTER
four
∗ ∗ ∗ ∗ ∗ ∗ ∗ ∗ ∗ ∗

Searching and Seizing People in Public Places

································ **DISCUSSION** ································

A t the beginning of the twentieth century, the Supreme Court believed that, as a general rule, police need a warrant to seize or search anyone or anything. Over time, however, the Court developed exceptions to this general principle. When it came to searching and seizing (arresting) people who were in public places, the Court ultimately decided a warrant generally would not be required.

The modern law concerning whether police need a search warrant or arrest warrant to search or arrest people in public places begins with the 1967 case of McCray v. Illinois (see p. 60). When a reliable informant told the police that George McCray had been selling drugs and that he had drugs in his possession, the police found McCray and searched him. After finding heroin in his pocket, they arrested him for possession of an illegal drug. The police did not obtain a search warrant before finding and searching George McCray.

Justice Stewart, writing for the majority in this five-to-four decision, stated that in general police do not need a search warrant to search people in a public place, but they do need probable cause. In proving probable cause, however, the police do not have to reveal the name of their informant. George McCray's conviction for possession of an illegal drug was upheld.

Justice Douglas dissented, joined by Justice Brennan, Justice Fortas, and Chief Justice Warren. He argued that police should be required to obtain a search warrant in most cases before they can search people in public places, with exceptions for emergency situations, such as where a crime is committed in the presence of a police officer. The police also should have to produce their informant in Court, he believed, so the attorney for the accused could cross-examine him or her.

The majority of justices thought that requiring a search warrant every time police wished to search someone in a public place would make law enforcement almost impossible. In their opinion, requiring police to have probable cause before making a search provided enough protection for the people being searched. The majority also accepted the argument that if the identities of informants were revealed there would be no more informants and law enforcement would become much more difficult.

NOT AN UNREASONABLE SEARCH OR SEIZURE

In 1973 the Court decided the case of *Cupp v. Murphy*. Justice Stewart wrote the opinion for the majority. Police brought Daniel Murphy to the police station for questioning after they found his wife dead. While the police did not know whether or not Daniel Murphy had killed his wife, they knew she had been strangled and there were scratch marks on her throat. Without a search warrant, the police took samples from under Murphy's fingernails.

The Court ruled that this search and seizure was reasonable under the circumstances. The police knew that if they did not act fast the evidence would be destroyed, so there was no time to obtain a search warrant. The police did have probable cause at the time to believe Murphy had killed his wife. The material under his fingernails turned out to be the skin and blood of Mrs. Murphy, and Daniel Murphy's conviction for her murder was upheld.

SEARCHES WITH ARRESTS

In another 1973 case, *United States v. Robinson*, Officer Richard Jenks, of the District of Columbia police force, pulled Willie Robinson's Cadillac over because Jenks had reason to believe Robinson's driver's license had expired. Jenks then arrested Robinson for driving without a valid driver's license, searched him, and found heroin in his possession, which led to Robinson's conviction for possession of an illegal drug.

Justice Rehnquist, who wrote the opinion for the Court, searched through ancient legal treatises for information about ancient English common law rules regarding when police may search people under similar circumstances, but he found little helpful information. Justice Rehnquist then traced the history of U.S. search and seizure law from the 1914 decision in *Weeks* to 1973 and also found little that would help to decide this particular case. May police search people when they arrest them? Justice Rehnquist and the majority thought that this should be allowed.

Justice Powell wrote a concurring opinion, in which he argued that once people are under arrest they do not have the same expectation of privacy as other people. In his opinion, it would only "frustrate law enforcement" to develop a set of complex rules to deal with this question. Willie Robinson's conviction would not be overturned.

The three dissenting justices, Douglas, Brennan, and Marshall, argued that a full search did not seem justified in this case because Robinson was being arrested for a minor traffic offense. Justice Marshall, in his dissenting opinion, suggested that in determining whether searches are justified in particular cases, the Court should rely on a case-by-case analysis, taking into consideration all the circumstances. The majority of justices did not want to get into the business of trying to draw the line between minor and major offenses. They also did not think a case-by-case approach would work in this area, because such an approach seemed like the road to more confusion for both the judges and the police. Instead, the Court ruled that whenever the police arrest someone they may search that person without a warrant.

ARREST IN A PUBLIC PLACE

In 1976 the Court finally decided whether an arrest warrant is required when someone is arrested in a public place. While the Court had ruled that an arrest warrant is usually required to arrest someone in a private place, such as a home or private office, did the same rule apply in a public place? Although this question seems so basic, before 1976 the Court had never been called upon to answer it. In *United States v. Watson,* a postal inspector received a telephone tip from an informant who claimed that Henry Watson was in possession of credit cards that had been stolen out of the mail. Postal inspectors then arrested Watson in a restaurant without first obtaining an arrest warrant.

Justice White pointed out that under the ancient English common law rules an arrest warrant was not required before someone could be arrested in a public place. The Fourth Amendment requires the police to be "reasonable," and it appeared, given this history, that it was not unreasonable to allow arrests to be made in public places without arrest warrants.

Justices Marshall and Brennan dissented, arguing that an arrest warrant should be required in most cases, with exceptions for a variety of situations. In 1976 the majority did not want to make a general arrest warrant requirement and then spend decades figuring out what the exceptions to that general requirement should be. That approach would probably confuse everyone involved, including those whose rights are protected by the Fourth Amendment. Henry Watson's conviction was upheld.

HOT PURSUIT

Also in 1976, the Court decided *United States v. Santana*, with Justice Rehnquist writing the opinion for the Court. When Michael Gilletti, an undercover officer with the Philadelphia Narcotics Squad, tried to make a heroin buy from Patricia McCafferty, she told him she would need $115 and that she would "go down to Mom Santana's for the dope." Officer Gilletti recorded the serial numbers of the marked bills and then gave them to McCafferty. After he received the drugs from McCafferty, he went to Mom Santana's house where he found her standing in the doorway. As he and other police officers came up to arrest her, Mom Santana retreated into the house. The police followed her into the house and arrested her.

The Court ruled that the police had probable cause to arrest Mom Santana in a public place, and when she retreated they had the right to follow her and make the arrest without a warrant. Police in "hot pursuit" of a fleeing felon do not need a warrant to enter a house or business. Justices Marshall and Brennan dissented, arguing that an arrest warrant should be required in most cases, whether the arrest is made on public or private property, but the majority was not prepared to restrict the police with such a requirement.

THE INVENTORY SEARCH

What if a person who is arrested has a bag or a briefcase? The 1983 case of *Illinois v. Lafayette* addressed this question. Police arrested Ralph Lafayette for disturbing the peace and took him to the police station. They then searched him and conducted an "inventory search" of his shoulder bag. As a result of the search, they found illegal drugs in the bag and added that to the charge.

Chief Justice Burger, who wrote the opinion for the unanimous Court, reviewed several Supreme Court decisions which held that police may conduct a search of property they impound to make sure it does not contain anything dangerous and to make a list of its contents so that the rightful owner can be assured nothing is missing when it is returned. Police routinely do inventory searches of automobiles, and the Court thought they should be able to do the same with shoulder bags and luggage taken to a police station. The police do not need a warrant or probable cause in order to conduct an inventory search, assuming the property they are searching is legally in their custody. Ralph Lafayette's conviction for the possession of illegal drugs was upheld.

SEARCHING INSIDE THE BODY

What if the police want to do more than a routine search? In 1985 the Court faced a difficult question in *Winston v. Lee*. The case involved a shopkeeper who had been wounded by a gunshot during an attempted robbery and also managed to wound the assailant. Police found Rudolph Lee bleeding from a gunshot wound a few blocks from the scene of the crime. They took him to the hospital, where the victim identified Rudolph Lee as the would-be robber. The police then asked a judge to order Rudolph Lee to undergo surgery to remove the bullet inside his body.

A unanimous Supreme Court overruled that order, stating that people have high expectations of privacy regarding what is inside their bodies. Justice Brennan, who wrote the opinion, argued that a balance must be struck between the type of intrusion and the need to conduct the search. In this case the police did not really need the bullet for evidence and the operation would be difficult and dangerous. Under these circumstances, the Court thought Rudolph Lee had a constitutional right to refuse to undergo surgery.

STOP AND FRISK

Beginning in 1968 the Court developed rules for when police may stop and frisk people without probable cause to believe they have committed a crime. Chief Justice Warren was able to write an opinion in the case of *Terry v. Ohio* (see p. 64) in which every justice joined except Justice Douglas. Detective McFadden of the Cleveland police department saw two suspicious characters standing on a downtown street corner. The men seemed to be "casing" a store for a possible robbery. They walked back and forth about two dozen times in front of the same store window. Hoping to prevent a robbery, Officer McFadden approached them and asked them their names. Before they could move he spun one of them, John Terry, around and patted him down, finding a pistol in a pocket. He also patted down Terry's companion, Richard Chilton, and found another pistol. Both Terry and Chilton were convicted of carrying concealed weapons.

The question for the Supreme Court was whether Officer McFadden had violated Terry's and Chilton's Fourth Amendment rights when he patted them down. Everyone involved with this case seemed to agree that Officer McFadden did not have probable cause to search the men at the moment he searched them. What Officer McFadden did have was a reasonable suspicion to believe these two were armed and dangerous. The Supreme Court had to determine whether or not police should be allowed to conduct this kind of search in order to protect themselves and the public.

Recognizing the dangerous world in which we live, the Court ruled that police may stop and frisk someone if they have a good reason to believe the person might be armed and dangerous. They do not have to wait until a crime is committed or until they have probable cause to arrest the person. Because of the limited nature of the search in this case it was "reasonable" to search these two suspicious characters. The Fourth Amendment, which outlaws unreasonable searches, had not been violated, so Terry's and Chilton's convictions would not be overturned.

In the 1979 case of *Ybarra v. Illinois*, Justice Rehnquist, Justice Blackmun, and Chief Justice Burger dissented from an opinion written by Justice Stewart. In this case police had a search warrant to search the Aurora Tap Tavern for drugs. While searching the tavern, the police also patted down the customers for weapons. When they frisked Ventura Ybarra, it was clear that he had a cigarette pack in his pocket. When they removed the pack they found that it contained illegal drugs. Ybarra was convicted for the possession of illegal drugs.

The Supreme Court threw out Ybarra's conviction. While *Terry* authorized police to frisk people in dangerous situations, the frisk was supposed to be a limited search for weapons. A cigarette pack is not a weapon and there was no reason for the police to think Ventura Ybarra was carrying drugs just because he was in the Aurora Tap Tavern. The *Terry* decision only authorizes a search for weapons if the police have reasonable suspicion to believe that someone is carrying a weapon. That decision does not give police a license to conduct a general search. In fact, the majority of justices thought that even the frisk for weapons was not reasonable in this case because there was no reason to believe Ybarra was carrying a weapon.

In 1989 the Court expanded the concept of what had come to be called the Terry stop in *United States v. Sokolow*. Chief Justice Rehnquist wrote the opinion for the majority. In this case, federal drug agents believed they had reasonable suspicion to stop and talk to Andrew Sokolow at the Honolulu airport long enough to allow a trained dog to sniff his luggage for illegal drugs. Andrew Sokolow had paid for his plane tickets with cash, traveled under an assumed name, stopped for a short time in Miami, appeared nervous, and had not checked any of his luggage. The Chief Justice ruled that, given these facts, these agents had reasonable suspicion to believe something was wrong, which was enough to justify stopping Sokolow long enough to talk to him and have a dog sniff his luggage.

Justices Marshall and Brennan dissented, arguing that police should have probable cause to make such a stop. They pointed out that *Terry* only authorized police to stop and frisk people they believed were armed and dangerous, and in this case the police did not believe Sokolow was either armed or dangerous. The majority of justices thought that police must be able to function in the real world and this search was not unreasonable behavior on their part. Sokolow's conviction for the possession of illegal drugs was upheld.

STOPPING PEOPLE WITHOUT CAUSE

In the 1979 case of *Brown v. Texas*, Chief Justice Burger was able to write an opinion from which no justice dissented. At 12:45 P.M. on the afternoon of December 9, 1977, Officers Venegas and Sotelo of the El Paso police department were cruising in their police car when they saw Zackary Brown in an alley. They asked him to identify himself and explain what he was doing in the alley but he refused. Although the police officers thought that Zackary Brown looked suspicious and he was in an area known for drug trafficking, they did not suspect him of any specific misconduct or have any reason to believe he was armed or dangerous. Zackary Brown refused to identify himself and said the police had no right to stop him. The police then frisked him and found nothing. They then arrested Zackary Brown for violation of Tex. Penal Code Title 8, Section 38.02 (a), which made it a criminal offense for a person who has been lawfully stopped by an officer to refuse to give his or her name and address if requested. Zackary Brown was ultimately fined $45 and appealed his case to the Supreme Court.

The Court ruled that when Zackary Brown was stopped by the police for questioning he had been seized under the Fourth Amendment. The police may only seize someone if they have probable cause to believe the person has committed a crime or reasonable suspicion to believe the person is armed and dangerous. Chief Justice Burger said it was necessary to strike a "balance between the public interest and the individual's right to personal security free from arbitrary interference by law officers." He believed that people's legitimate expectation of privacy should not be subject to "arbitrary invasions solely at the unfettered discretion of officers in the field." The police must have specific objective facts that form the basis of their reason for the stop. They must at least have "reasonable suspicion, based on objective facts, that the individual is involved in criminal activity." There was no reasonable suspicion in this case. Brown was simply walking down an alley and that does not form the basis for reasonable suspicion. Brown got his $45 back.

JUDICIAL REVIEW OF WARRANTLESS ARRESTS

By 1990 the basic rules of what police can and cannot do with people who are in public places seemed clear. Police do not need a warrant to search or arrest a person, but they do need probable cause in most situations. Also, if someone is arrested without an arrest warrant, he or she must be brought before a judge "promptly" for a hearing to determine whether the police had probable cause to make the arrest. The problem for judges and police departments was trying to decide what "promptly" meant. Finally, in 1991, the Supreme Court provided an answer to that question in the case of *County of Riverside v. McLaughlin.*

Justice O'Connor, who wrote the opinion for the five-justice majority, pointed out that she and the majority of justices understood the need for a definite rule because former rulings on the subject had led to nothing but confusion. The majority thought that someone arrested without a warrant should be brought before a judge within 48 hours for judicial review of whether the police had probable cause to make the arrest. The Court believed that this would strike a reasonable balance between the practical needs of law enforcement and the rights of the individual. Justice O'Connor went on to say:

> [A]lthough we hesitate to announce that the Constitution compels a specific time limit, it is important to provide some degree of certainty so that States and counties may establish procedures with confidence that they fall within constitutional bounds.

The 48-hour rule became the new constitutional standard.

The four dissenting justices argued that 48 hours is too long and that the time allowed should depend on the circumstances of each case. The majority of justices disagreed. They had seen the problems caused by leaving issues such as this up to the circumstances of each case and believed that even if some people were held longer than absolutely necessary everyone involved in the criminal justice system, from the police to those accused of crime, would benefit from a definite rule.

SEARCHES IN SCHOOLS

The case of *New Jersey v. T.L.O.*, decided in 1985, involved the right of public school children to be free from unreasonable searches and seizures. All of the justices agreed that the Fourth Amendment did apply to the public school setting, but they disagreed on the extent of this application. Justice White wrote the opinion for the majority. The case involved a 14-year-old girl caught smoking in the school bathroom. When the assistant vice principal opened the girl's purse, he found marijuana. The girl was then subjected to delinquency charges in juvenile court. The question before the Supreme Court was whether or not the Fourth Amendment and the exclusionary rule should be applied in this case.

Justice White ruled that students in public schools are protected by the Fourth Amendment. At the same time, a balance must be struck between the student's legitimate expectation of privacy and the school's need to maintain an environment of learning. School officials would not be required to obtain a search warrant or even have probable cause before searching a student. However, they would need to have what Justice White called a "reasonable suspicion" to believe the search would produce the evidence sought. The assistant vice principal had reasonable suspicion to believe that the purse contained cigarettes in violation of school rules. When he opened the purse and found marijuana, he was acting reasonably under the circumstances. Justice White thought that a search in a public school must be reasonable, meaning it must be justified and carried out in a reasonable way. He ruled that the search of this student's purse was reasonable in this case. Justices Brennan, Marshall, and Stevens dissented, arguing that the majority's opinion gave too much power to school officials to ignore the requirements of the Fourth Amendment.

This decision was a significant break with the past. Until 1985 school officials argued that they had the same power to search students that parents have, based on an ancient doctrine that teachers stand *in loco parentis* (in the place of the parents). The Court rejected this idea, finding public school officials to be government officials covered by the Fourth Amendment and students to be people protected by the Fourth Amendment.

CONCLUSION

The Supreme Court did not begin to develop the rules concerning when people in public places could be searched and seized until after the news media highlighted the confused state of the law in this area. The result has been a Court ever mindful of the need for uncomplicated rules that do not hang on a thousand factors and are not dependent on a case-by-case analysis. The rules the Court has developed are simple and straightforward.

Police generally need probable cause to arrest or search someone in a public place. They do not need a warrant, but within 48 hours after an arrest made without an arrest warrant, they must bring the person who has been arrested before a judge. The police may conduct an inventory search of any luggage or bags the arrested person has with him or her, but this procedure must be performed consistently. In other words, everything must be subject to the same inventory search. An inventory search cannot be used with some people and not with other people.

When people are in a private place, a warrant will generally be required before they can be arrested or searched. People in a public place may be stopped and frisked in situations where it is reasonable to believe they might be armed and dangerous. However, police may not stop people and ask for identification if there is no reason to suspect them of having violated the law.

.............................CASE DECISIONS...

McCray v. Illinois concerned the arrest and search of a person in a public place. A majority of justices ruled that police could make this arrest and conduct this search with probable cause and without a warrant. They also ruled that police did not have to reveal the name of the informant who provided them with the information which constituted probable cause. Justice Stewart wrote the opinion for the majority, which is included here. Justice Douglas's dissenting opinion is also included.

The extent to which police may stop and frisk suspicious people who are in public and may be armed and dangerous was the issue the Court faced in *Terry v. Ohio*. The majority ruled that police may stop and frisk such people without probable cause if the police have a reasonable suspicion that the people pose a threat to public safety. Chief Justice Warren wrote the majority opinion, which is included here. Justices Black, Harlan, and White wrote concurring opinions and Justice Douglas wrote a dissenting opinion, none of which are included here.

Following are excerpts from the case decisions.

❈ ❈ ❈ ❈ ❈ ❈ ❈ ❈

McCRAY v. ILLINOIS
386 U.S. 300 (1967)

Mr. Justice Stewart delivered the opinion of the Court.

The petitioner was arrested in Chicago, Illinois, on the morning of January 16, 1964, for possession of narcotics. The Chicago police officers who made the arrest found a package containing heroin on his person and he was indicted for its unlawful possession. Prior to trial he filed a motion to suppress the heroin as evidence against him, claiming that the police had acquired it in an unlawful search and seizure in violation of the Fourth and Fourteenth Amendments. See *Mapp v. Ohio*, 367 U.S. 643. After a hearing, the court denied the motion, and the petitioner was subsequently convicted upon the evidence of the heroin the arresting officers had found in his possession. The judgment of conviction was affirmed by the Supreme Court of Illinois, and we granted certiorari to consider the petitioner's claim that the hearing on his motion to suppress was constitutionally defective.

The petitioner's arrest occurred near the intersection of 49th Street and Calumet Avenue at about seven in the morning. At the hearing on the motion to suppress, he testified that up until a half hour before he was arrested he had been at "a friend's house" about a block away, that after leaving the friend's house he had "walked with a lady from 48th to 48th and South Park," and that, as he approached 49th Street and Calumet Avenue, "[t]he Officers stopped me going through the alley." "The officers," he said, "did not show me a search warrant for my person or an arrest warrant for my arrest." He said the officers then searched him and found the narcotics in question. The petitioner did not identify the "friend" or the "lady," and neither of them appeared as a witness.

The arresting officers then testified. Officer Jackson stated that he and two fellow officers had had a conversation with an informant on the morning of January 16 in their unmarked police car. The officer said that the informant had told them that the petitioner, with whom Jackson was acquainted, "was selling narcotics and had narcotics on his person and that he could be found in the vicinity of 47th and Calumet at this particular time." Jackson said that he and his fellow officers drove to that vicinity in the police car and that when they spotted the petitioner, the informant pointed him out and then departed on foot. Jackson stated that the officers observed the petitioner walking with a woman, then separating from her and meeting briefly with a man, then proceeding alone, and finally, after seeing the police car, "hurriedly walk[ing] between two buildings." "At this point," Jackson testified, "my partner and myself got out of the car and informed him we had information he had narcotics on his person, placed him in the police vehicle at this point." Jackson stated that the officers then searched the petitioner and found the heroin in a cigarette package.

Jackson testified that he had been acquainted with the informant for approximately a year, that during this period the informant had supplied him with information about narcotics activities "fifteen, sixteen times at least," that the information had proved to be accurate and had resulted in numerous arrests and convictions. On cross-examination, Jackson was even more specific as to the informant's previous reliability, giving the names of people who had been convicted of narcotics violations as the result of information the informant had supplied. When Jackson was asked for the informant's name and address, counsel for the State objected, and the objection was sustained by the court. . . .

There can be no doubt, upon the basis of the circumstances related by Officers Jackson and Arnold, that there was probable cause to sustain the arrest and incidental search in this case. *Draper v. United States*, 358 U.S. 307. Unlike the situation in *Beck v. Ohio*, 379 U.S. 89, each of the officers in this case described with specificity "what the informer actually said, and why the officer thought the information was credible." 379 U.S., at 97. The testimony of each of the officers informed the court of the "underlying circumstances from which the informant concluded that the narcotics were where he claimed they were, and some of the underlying circumstances from which the officer concluded that the informant . . . was 'credible' or his information 'reliable.' " *Aguilar v. Texas*, 378 U.S. 108, 114. See *United States v. Ventresca*, 380 U.S. 102. Upon the basis of those circumstances, along with the officers' personal observations of the petitioner, the court was fully justified in holding that at the time the officers made the arrest "the facts and circumstances within their knowledge and of which they had reasonably trustworthy information were sufficient to warrant a prudent man in believing that the petitioner had committed or was committing an offense. *Brinegar v. United States*, 338 U.S. 160, 175–176; *Henry v. United States*, 361 U.S. 98, 102." *Beck v. Ohio, supra*, at 91. It is the petitioner's claim, however, that even though the officers' sworn testimony fully supported a finding of probable cause for the arrest and search, the state court nonetheless violated the Constitution when it sustained objections to the petitioner's questions as to the identity of the informant. We cannot agree.

In permitting the officers to withhold the informant's identity, the court was following well-settled Illinois law. When the issue is not guilt or innocence, but, as here, the question of probable cause for an arrest or search, the Illinois Supreme Court has held that police officers need not invariably be required to disclose an informant's identity if the trial judge is convinced, by evidence submitted in open court and subject to cross-examination, that the officers did rely in good faith upon credible information supplied by a reliable informant. This Illinois evidentiary rule is consistent with the law of many other States. . . .

In sum, the Court in the exercise of its power to formulate evidentiary rules for federal criminal cases has consistently declined to hold that an informer's identity need always be disclosed in a federal criminal trial, let alone in a preliminary hearing to determine probable cause for an arrest or search. Yet we are now asked to hold that the Constitution somehow compels Illinois to abolish the informer's privilege from its law of evidence, and to require disclosure of the informer's identity in every such preliminary hearing where it appears that the officers made the arrest or search in reliance upon facts supplied by an informer they had reason to trust. The argument is based upon the Due Process Clause of the Fourteenth Amendment, and upon the Sixth Amendment right of confrontation, applicable to the States through the Fourteenth Amendment. *Pointer v. Texas*, 380 U.S. 400. We find no support for the petitioner's position in either of those constitutional provisions.

Dissenting Opinion   MR. JUSTICE DOUGLAS, with whom THE CHIEF JUSTICE, MR. JUSTICE BRENNAN and MR. JUSTICE FORTAS concur, dissenting.

We have here a Fourth Amendment question concerning the validity of an arrest. If the police see a crime being committed they can of course seize the culprit. If a person is fleeing the scene of a crime, the police can stop him. And there are cases of "hot pursuit" and other instances of probable cause when the police can make an arrest. But normally an arrest should be made only on a warrant issued by a magistrate on a showing of "probable cause, supported by oath or affirmation," as required by the Fourth Amendment. At least since *Mapp v. Ohio*, 367 U.S. 643, the States are as much bound by those provisions as is the Federal Government. But for the Fourth Amendment they could fashion the rule for arrests that the Court now approves. With all deference, the requirements of the Fourth Amendment now make that conclusion unconstitutional.

No warrant for the arrest of petitioner was obtained in this case. The police, instead of going to a magistrate and making a showing of "probable cause" based on their informant's tip-off, acted on their own. They, rather than the magistrate, became the arbiters of "probable cause." The Court's approval of that process effectively rewrites the Fourth Amendment. . . .

There is no way to determine the reliability of Old Reliable, the informer, unless he is produced at the trial and cross-examined. Unless he is produced, the Fourth Amendment is entrusted to the tender mercies of the police. What we do today is to encourage arrests and searches without warrants. The whole momentum of criminal law administration should be in precisely the opposite direction, if the Fourth Amendment is to remain a vital force. Except in rare and emergency cases, it requires magistrates to make the findings of "probable cause." We should be mindful of its command that a judicial mind should be interposed between the police and the citizen. We should also be mindful that "disclosure, rather than suppression, of relevant materials ordinarily promotes the proper administration of criminal justice." *Dennis v. United States*, 384 U.S. 855, 870.

TERRY v. OHIO
392 U.S. 1 (1968)

MR. CHIEF JUSTICE WARREN delivered the opinion of the Court.

This case presents serious questions concerning the role of the Fourth Amendment in the confrontation on the street between the citizen and the policeman investigating suspicious circumstances.

Petitioner Terry was convicted of carrying a concealed weapon and sentenced to the statutorily prescribed term of one to three years in the penitentiary. Following the denial of a pretrial motion to suppress, the prosecution introduced in evidence two revolvers and a number of bullets seized from Terry and a codefendant, Richard Chilton, by Cleveland Police Detective Martin McFadden. At the hearing on the motion to suppress this evidence, Officer McFadden testified that while he was patrolling in plain clothes in downtown Cleveland at approximately 2:30 in the afternoon of October 31, 1963, his attention was attracted by two men, Chilton and Terry, standing on the corner of Huron Road and Euclid Avenue. He had never seen the two men before, and he was unable to say precisely what first drew his eye to them. However, he testified that he had been a policeman for 39 years and a detective for 35 and that he had been assigned to patrol this vicinity of downtown Cleveland for shoplifters and pickpockets for 30 years. He explained that he had developed routine habits of observation over the years and that he would "stand and watch people or walk and watch people at many intervals of the day." He added: "Now, in this case when I looked over they didn't look right to me at the time."

His interest aroused, Officer McFadden took up a post of observation in the entrance to a store 300 to 400 feet away from the two men. "I get more purpose to watch them when I seen their movements," he testified. He saw one of the men leave the other one and walk southwest on Huron Road, past some stores. The man paused for a moment and looked in a store window, then walked on a short distance, turned around and walked back toward the corner, pausing once again to look in the same store window. He rejoined his companion at the corner, and the two conferred briefly. Then the second man went through the same series of motions, strolling down Huron Road, looking in the same window, walking on a short distance, turning back, peering in the store window again, and returning to confer with the first man at the corner. The two men repeated this ritual alternately between five and six times apiece—in all, roughly a dozen trips. At one point, while the two were standing together on the corner, a third man approached them and engaged them briefly in conversation. This man then left the two others and walked west on Euclid Avenue. Chilton and Terry resumed their measured pacing, peering, and conferring. After this had gone on for 10 to 12 minutes, the two men walked off together, heading west on Euclid Avenue, following the path taken earlier by the third man.

By this time Officer McFadden had become thoroughly suspicious. He testified that after observing their elaborately casual and oft-repeated reconnaissance of the store window on Huron Road, he suspected the two men of "casing a job, a stick-up," and that he considered it his duty as a police officer to investigate further. He added that he feared "they may have a gun." Thus, Officer McFadden followed Chilton and Terry and saw them stop in front of Zucker's store to talk to the same man who had conferred with them earlier on the street corner. Deciding that the situation was ripe for direct action, Officer McFadden approached the three men, identified himself as a police officer and asked for their names. At this point his knowledge was confined to what he had observed. He was not acquainted with any of the three men by name or by sight, and he had received no information concerning them from any other source. When the men "mumbled something" in response to his inquiries, Officer McFadden grabbed petitioner Terry, spun him around so that they were facing the other two, with Terry between McFadden and the others, and patted down the outside of his clothing. In the left breast pocket of Terry's overcoat Officer McFadden felt a pistol. He reached inside the overcoat pocket, but was unable to remove the gun. At this point, keeping Terry between himself and the others, the officer ordered all three men to enter Zucker's store. As they went in, he removed Terry's overcoat completely, removed a .38-caliber revolver from the pocket and ordered all three men to face the wall with their hands raised. Officer McFadden proceeded to pat down the outer clothing of Chilton and the third man, Katz. He discovered another revolver in the outer pocket of Chilton's overcoat, but no weapons were found on Katz. The officer testified that he only patted the men down to see whether they had weapons, and that he did not put his hands beneath the outer garments of either Terry or Chilton until he felt their guns. So far as appears from the record, he never placed his hands beneath Katz' outer garments. Officer McFadden seized Chilton's gun, asked the proprietor of the store to call a police wagon, and took all three men to the station, where Chilton and Terry were formally charged with carrying concealed weapons.

On the motion to suppress the guns the prosecution took the position that they had been seized following a search incident to a lawful arrest. The trial court rejected this theory, stating that it "would be stretching the facts beyond reasonable comprehension" to find that Officer McFadden had had probable cause to arrest the men before he patted them down for weapons. However, the court denied the defendants' motion on the ground that Officer McFadden, on the basis of his experience, "had reasonable cause to believe . . . that the defendants were conducting themselves suspiciously, and some interrogation should be made of their action." Purely for his own protection, the court held, the officer had the right to pat down the outer clothing of these men, who he had reasonable cause to believe might be armed. The court distinguished between an investigatory "stop" and an arrest, and between a "frisk" of the outer clothing for weapons and a full-blown search for evidence of crime. The frisk, it held, was essential to the proper performance of the officer's investigatory duties, for without it "the answer to the police officer may be a bullet, and a loaded pistol discovered during the frisk is admissible."

After the court denied their motion to suppress, Chilton and Terry waived jury trial and pleaded not guilty. The court adjudged them guilty, and the Court of Appeals for the Eighth Judicial District, Cuyahoga County, affirmed. *State v. Terry*, 5 Ohio App. 2d 122, 214 N.E. 2d 114 (1966). The Supreme Court of Ohio dismissed their appeal on the ground that no "substantial constitutional question" was involved. We granted certiorari, 387 U.S. 929 (1967), to determine whether the admission of the revolvers in evidence violated petitioner's rights under the Fourth Amendment, made applicable to the States by the Fourteenth. *Mapp v. Ohio*, 367 U.S. 643 (1961). We affirm the conviction. . . .

We have recently held that "the Fourth Amendment protects people, not places," *Katz v. United States*, 389 U.S. 347, 351 (1967), and wherever an individual may harbor a reasonable "expectation of privacy," *id.*, at 361 (Mr. Justice Harlan, concurring), he is entitled to be free from unreasonable governmental intrusion. Of course, the specific content and incidents of this right must be shaped by the context in which it is asserted. For "what the Constitution forbids is not all searches and seizures, but unreasonable searches and seizures." *Elkins v. United States*, 364 U.S. 206, 222 (1960). Unquestionably petitioner was entitled to the protection of the Fourth Amendment as he walked down the street in Cleveland. . . . The question is whether in all the circumstances of this on-the-street encounter, his right to personal security was violated by an unreasonable search and seizure. . . .

Our first task is to establish at what point in this encounter the Fourth Amendment becomes relevant. That is, we must decide whether and when Officer McFadden "seized" Terry and whether and when he conducted a "search." There is some suggestion in the use of such terms as "stop" and "frisk" that such police conduct is outside the purview of the Fourth Amendment because neither action rises to the level of a "search" or "seizure" within the meaning of the Constitution. We emphatically reject this notion. It is quite plain that the Fourth Amendment governs "seizures" of the person which do not eventuate in a trip to the station house and prosecution for crime—"arrests" in traditional terminology. It must be recognized that whenever a police officer accosts an individual and restrains his freedom to walk away, he has "seized" that person. And it is nothing less than sheer torture of the English language to suggest that a careful exploration of the outer surfaces of a person's clothing all over his or her body in an attempt to find weapons is not a "search." . . .

The danger in the logic which proceeds upon distinctions between a "stop" and an "arrest," or "seizure" of the person, and between a "frisk" and a "search" is two-fold. It seeks to isolate from constitutional scrutiny the initial stages of the contact between the policeman and the citizen. And by suggesting a rigid all-or-nothing model of justification and regulation under the Amendment, it obscures the utility of limitations upon the scope, as well as the initiation, of police action as a means of constitutional regulation. This Court has held in the past that a search which is reasonable at its inception may violate the Fourth Amendment by virtue of its intolerable intensity and scope. . . .

The distinctions of classical "stop-and-frisk" theory thus serve to divert attention from the central inquiry under the Fourth Amendment—the reasonableness in all the circumstances of the particular governmental invasion of a citizen's personal security. "Search" and "seizure" are not talismans. We therefore reject the notions that the Fourth Amendment does not come into play at all as a limitation upon police conduct if the officers stop short of something called a "technical arrest" or a "full-blown search."

In this case there can be no question, then, that Officer McFadden "seized" petitioner and subjected him to a "search" when he took hold of him and patted down the outer surfaces of his clothing. We must decide whether at that point it was reasonable for Officer McFadden to have interfered with petitioner's personal security as he did. And in determining whether the seizure and search were "unreasonable" our inquiry is a dual one—whether the officer's action was justified at its inception, and whether it was reasonably related in scope to the circumstances which justified the interference in the first place. . . .

The crux of this case, however, is not the propriety of Officer McFadden's taking steps to investigate petitioner's suspicious behavior, but rather, whether there was justification for McFadden's invasion of Terry's personal security by searching him for weapons in the course of that investigation. We are now concerned with more than the governmental interest in investigating crime; in addition, there is the more immediate interest of the police officer in taking steps to assure himself that the person with whom he is dealing is not armed with a weapon that could unexpectedly and fatally be used against him. Certainly it would be unreasonable to require that police officers take unnecessary risks in the performance of their duties. American criminals have a long tradition of armed violence, and every year in this country many law enforcement officers are killed in the line of duty, and thousands more are wounded. Virtually all of these deaths and a substantial portion of the injuries are inflicted with guns and knives.

In view of these facts, we cannot blind ourselves to the need for law enforcement officers to protect themselves and other prospective victims of violence in situations where they may lack probable cause for an arrest. When an officer is justified in believing that the individual whose suspicious behavior he is investigating at close range is armed and presently dangerous to the officer or to others, it would appear to be clearly unreasonable to deny the officer the power to take necessary measures to determine whether the person is in fact carrying a weapon and to neutralize the threat of physical harm. . . .

We need not develop at length in this case, however, the limitations which the Fourth Amendment places upon a protective seizure and search for weapons. These limitations will have to be developed in the concrete factual circumstances of individual cases. . . . Suffice it to note that such a search, unlike a search without a warrant incident to a lawful arrest, is not justified by any need to prevent the disappearance or destruction of evidence of crime. See *Preston v. United States*, 376 U.S. 364, 367 (1964). The sole justification of the search in the present situation is the protection of the police officer and others nearby, and it must therefore be confined in scope to an intrusion reasonably designed to discover guns, knives, clubs, or other hidden instruments for the assault of the police officer.

The scope of the search in this case presents no serious problem in light of these standards. Officer McFadden patted down the outer clothing of petitioner and his two companions. He did not place his hands in their pockets or under the outer surface of their garments until he had felt weapons, and then he merely reached for and removed the guns. He never did invade Katz' person beyond the outer surfaces of his clothes, since he discovered nothing in his pat-down which might have been a weapon. Officer McFadden confined his search strictly to what was minimally necessary to learn whether the men were armed and to disarm them once he discovered the weapons. He did not conduct a general exploratory search for whatever evidence of criminal activity he might find.

We conclude that the revolver seized from Terry was properly admitted in evidence against him. At the time he seized petitioner and searched him for weapons, Officer McFadden had reasonable grounds to believe that petitioner was armed and dangerous, and it was necessary for the protection of himself and others to take swift measures to discover the true facts and neutralize the threat of harm if it materialized. The policeman carefully restricted his search to what was appropriate to the discovery of the particular items which he sought. Each case of this sort will, of course, have to be decided on its own facts. We merely hold today that where a police officer observes unusual conduct which leads him reasonably to conclude in light of his experience that criminal activity may be afoot and that the persons with whom he is dealing may be armed and presently dangerous, where in the course of investigating this behavior he identifies himself as a policeman and makes reasonable inquiries, and where nothing in the initial stages of the encounter serves to dispel his reasonable fear for his own or others' safety, he is entitled for the protection of himself and others in the area to conduct a carefully limited search of the outer clothing of such persons in an attempt to discover weapons which might be used to assault him. Such a search is a reasonable search under the Fourth Amendment, and any weapons seized may properly be introduced in evidence against the person from whom they were taken.

Affirmed.

.... DISCUSSION QUESTIONS ....

1. In 1967, by a five-to-four vote, the Supreme Court ruled that police do not need a search warrant to search people in public places. How would law enforcement procedures be different if the vote had been five-to-four the other way?

2. In a variety of circumstances police may pat down suspects even if the police do not have probable cause for a full search or arrest. What circumstances?

3. When arresting someone, police may search the person and the area in his or her immediate control. How far away from the person do you think this search can go? Do you think this search of the surrounding area is justified? Why?

4. The Court has ruled that police do not need an arrest warrant to arrest someone in a public place, and that an arrest warrant only justifies searching the suspect's home for the suspect. Do you think police will bother to get an arrest warrant in most cases? When would they bother to do so?

5. Police do not have the right to ask for a person's name and identification unless they have "probable cause" or "reasonable suspicion." Do you agree with this decision? How is asking a person for his or her name and identification an unreasonable search or seizure?

6. In the 1985 decision in *New Jersey v. T.L.O.*, the Court ruled that public school officials do not need probable cause or a warrant before they may search students, only reasonable suspicion. What do you think about this decision?

CHAPTER
five
❋ ❋ ❋ ❋ ❋ ❋ ❋ ❋ ❋

Searching and Seizing
Automobiles and Baggage

DISCUSSION

By 1925 the U.S. Supreme Court had clearly decided that the Fourth Amendment required federal police officers to have a warrant before entering a home or the private area of a business. Later, when the Court determined that the Fourteenth Amendment made the Fourth Amendment applicable to the states, this same rule applied to state and local police officers. Next, the Court tried to develop a rule concerning police searches of automobiles that struck the right balance between the needs of law enforcement and the privacy rights of citizens. The main issue was determining when police need a search warrant before they may search or seize an automobile.

SEARCHING AUTOMOBILES

In the 1925 case of *Carroll v. United States* (see p. 83), the Court for the first time applied the Fourth Amendment to the search of an automobile. The case involved the Carroll brothers, notorious bootleggers in Michigan, who were generally known to sell illegal liquor in the Grand Rapids area. When federal agents saw the Carroll brothers driving in the direction of Grand Rapids from Detroit, a known source of illegal liquor smuggled in from Canada, they stopped the Carrolls' car and searched it. Under the upholstery in the back seat the federal agents found cases of liquor. The Carroll brothers were convicted of violating the National Prohibition Act.

The Carroll brothers' attorney argued that the federal agents should have obtained a search warrant before stopping and searching the car. A unanimous Court decided that no search warrant was required in this situation. Chief Justice Taft wrote the opinion for the Court. He declared:

> [I]f the search and seizure without a warrant are made upon probable cause, that is, upon a belief, reasonably arising out of circumstances known to the seizing officer, that an automobile or other vehicle contains that which by law is subject to seizure and destruction, the search and seizure are valid. The Fourth Amendment is to be construed in the light of what was deemed an unreasonable search and seizure when it was adopted, and in a manner which will conserve public interests as well as the interests and rights of individual citizens.

Chief Justice Taft thought that requiring police to have a warrant to seize and search an automobile on the open road would neither fulfill the original intent of the authors of the Fourth Amendment nor serve the legitimate interests of modern law enforcement.

After reviewing the many laws Congress had passed on the subject of search and seizure since the adoption of the Fourth Amendment, the chief justice found that in the opinion of Congress a warrant was generally required only when a building was to be searched. He said:

> [T]he guaranty of freedom from unreasonable searches and seizures by the Fourth Amendment has been construed, practically since the beginning of the Government, as recognizing a necessary difference between a search of a store, dwelling house or other structure in respect of which a proper official warrant readily may be obtained, and a search of a ship, motor boat, wagon or automobile, for contraband goods, where it is not practicable to secure a warrant because the vehicle can be quickly moved out of the locality or jurisdiction in which the warrant must be sought.

At the same time Chief Justice Taft rejected the idea that federal agents could stop and search automobiles at will without probable cause. It would be "intolerable and unreasonable," he argued, for federal agents to stop every automobile "on the chance of finding liquor and thus subject all persons lawfully using the highways to the inconvenience and indignity of such a search."

Chief Justice Taft believed the line he was drawing between buildings and automobiles was a reasonable one and would further the interests protected by the Fourth Amendment as well as the need for effective law enforcement. He went on to say:

> We here find the line of distinction between legal and illegal seizures of liquor in transport in vehicles. It is certainly a reasonable distinction. It gives the owner of an automobile or other vehicle seized under Section

26, in absence of probable cause, a right to have restored to him the automobile, it protects him under the *Weeks* and *Amos* cases from use of the liquor as evidence against him, and it subjects the officer making the seizures to [a suit for] damages.

For later Courts, the problem with Chief Justice Taft's decision in *Carroll* is that he did not stop there. Instead, he made a general statement that would haunt the Supreme Court for generations to come. He said that the Fourth Amendment required officers to obtain a search warrant whenever it was "reasonably practicable" to obtain one. In cases where it is "impossible" to obtain a warrant, he continued, the officer may act, but only if probable cause exists. Chief Justice Taft hoped that this would provide a rule that would be "easily applied and understood," but that would not be the case. The expansive language requiring a warrant whenever "practicable" and only allowing a search or seizure without a warrant if it is "impossible" to get a warrant forced future Courts to search high and low for rules that would live up to that language without making law enforcement all but impossible in the modern world.

DEFINING PROBABLE CAUSE

While the members of this 1925 Supreme Court agreed that a warrant was not required in *Carroll*, they differed over whether the federal agents involved actually had probable cause to make this search. Seven justices believed that the agents did have probable cause. After all, the Carroll brothers were notorious bootleggers in Grand Rapids, and Detroit was located along an international border where liquor was known to come into the country. The Carroll brothers were driving from Detroit to Grand Rapids. For seven justices, that was enough to constitute probable cause to stop and search their car.

Justices McReynolds and Sutherland did not agree and wrote a dissenting opinion. In their view, the Carroll brothers were stopped by federal agents "while quietly driving an ordinary automobile along a much frequented public road." This was not, in their opinion, enough to justify either the stop or the search. They argued that "the facts known by the officers . . . were wholly insufficient to create a reasonable belief" that the Carroll brothers were transporting illegal liquor at that moment in time. The seven-justice majority did not agree, and the conviction of the Carroll brothers was upheld.

In 1959, in the case of *Henry v. United States*, the Warren Court began to move away from the *Carroll* decision, over the dissenting opinions of Chief Justice Warren and Justice Clark. Justice Douglas wrote the opinion for the majority. The case involved cases of whiskey (which was perfectly legal by this time) that were stolen while in interstate shipment. Two federal agents had seen John Henry in the area of the theft with someone the agents suspected of having stolen the whiskey. They followed John Henry and saw him putting cases of something into a car, but they were too far away to see whether the cases contained whiskey. The agents stopped Henry's car and searched it, finding some of the stolen cases of whiskey. John Henry was convicted of possession of property stolen while in interstate shipment.

A majority of the Supreme Court justices did not believe these agents had probable cause to stop Henry's car given these facts. While the agents suspected that Henry was involved in the theft, suspicion was not enough. Henry had no criminal record before this stop, and simply talking to someone and putting something into a car was not enough to create probable cause. Henry's conviction was overturned.

WARRANTS AND AUTOMOBILE SEARCHES

In 1964, in the case of *Preston v. United States*, the Court for the first time made a distinction between seizing a car and searching it. Police in Newport, Kentucky, received a phone call at 3:00 A.M. alerting them that three suspicious men had been sitting in a car all night in the downtown area. When they confronted these men, the police found that the men were all unemployed and only had 25 cents among them. The police then arrested all three for vagrancy, towed the car to a garage, and searched the car. They found guns, ropes, caps, women's stockings, pillow slips, and illegal license plates—everything necessary to pull off a bank robbery. After the search, one of the men confessed that they had intended to rob a bank.

A unanimous Supreme Court, in an opinion by Justice Black, ruled that if the police had time to tow the car to a garage they also had time to obtain a search warrant. While the police might have had probable cause to seize the car and its occupants (this was not really discussed), they should have obtained a search warrant before going further and searching the automobile because the Fourth Amendment protects privacy as well as property. For this reason, the convictions for conspiracy to rob a bank were overturned.

Just six years later, in *Chambers v. Maroney*, the Court seemed to overturn the *Preston* decision with only one dissenter, Justice Harlan. Justice White wrote the opinion for the majority. On the night of May 20, 1963, in North Braddock, Pennsylvania, two men committed armed robbery of a gas station. Witnesses saw a blue station wagon near the gas station at the time of the robbery. Soon after the robbery, police stopped a blue station wagon and took it to the police station. A search revealed two revolvers, change, and a card from the gas station that had been robbed. The two men caught in the station wagon were convicted on this evidence. Their attorney argued that under the ruling in *Preston* the police should have gotten a search warrant once they had the station wagon in custody.

The majority of justices did not agree. They thought the police had probable cause to arrest these two and search their automobile while making the arrest. If the police could search the car on the open road, then why penalize them for moving the car before searching it? To Justice White and most members of the Court, this distinction between a search in the field and one in the station seemed to be overly technical and to serve no real purpose except to force police to search cars on the highway instead of in the police garage. What important Fourth Amendment goal did that requirement further? The convictions in this case were upheld. As a general rule, police did not need a search warrant to stop and search an automobile.

Justice Harlan dissented, arguing that the general rule had been, and still was, that police should get a search warrant if practical. Certainly it was practical once the car had been moved into police custody. None of the justices discussed the distinction between seizing and searching. Back in 1925, the justices who decided the *Carroll* case apparently assumed that once a car had been seized the police could search it; these justices would probably have found it strange that police could seize something but not then search. In 1970, in *Chambers*, however, this distinction did not seem strange because of the Warren Court's focus on privacy rights as opposed to property rights.

Under the Burger Court the issue of when police could search automobiles without a warrant got more complex and confusing. The 1971 case of *Coolidge v. New Hampshire* concerned Pamela Mason, a 14-year-old girl who left her home in Manchester, New Hampshire, on the night of January 13, 1964, during a heavy snowstorm, apparently in response to a man's telephone call asking her to be a baby-sitter. Eight days later, when the snow melted, her dead body was found. The state police began an intensive investigation to find her killer. On January 28, 1964, they learned from a neighbor that Edward Coolidge had been away from his home the evening Pamela Mason disappeared. Edward Coolidge agreed to take a lie detector test and claimed he had nothing to do with the girl's death.

The police then asked the New Hampshire attorney general to issue a search warrant for Coolidge's house and automobiles, which the attorney general signed in his capacity as a justice of the peace. The cars, which the police found parked in front of Coolidge's house, were then towed to the police station and searched carefully. Coolidge was later convicted and sentenced to life in prison based on material vacuumed up from the inside of his 1951 Pontiac.

The Supreme Court threw out the conviction after determining that the warrant was no good because it had been issued by a law enforcement officer rather than by a "neutral and detached" judicial officer. The New Hampshire attorney general argued that the police did not need a warrant to bring this car into the police station for a search because they had probable cause and the Court had ruled in *Chambers* that police did not need a warrant when an automobile was involved.

The five-justice majority, in an opinion by Justice Stewart, rejected this argument. These justices ruled that a warrant is required unless one of the exceptions to the warrant requirement applies. The majority of justices thought that the so-called automobile exception only applied to automobiles that were stopped on the highway. Coolidge's 1951 Pontiac was parked in his driveway. The Court could have avoided a lot of confusion if it had ruled that the car was a part of the "curtilage" in this case, but it did not. It simply argued that the general warrant requirement should apply in this case because the car was not stopped on the open road.

Chief Justice Burger and Justices White, Black, and Blackmun dissented from part of the decision. While they agreed that this warrant was not valid because it had not been issued by a neutral and detached magistrate, they did not believe that a warrant was required in this case. In his dissenting opinion, Justice White pointed out that in reviewing past decisions by the Court concerning automobiles no "trick of logic will make them all perfectly consistent." He did not think drawing a distinction between an automobile parked in a driveway and one parked on the street served any real purpose.

Justice Harlan wrote a concurring opinion in which he noted that everyone involved in the crime-fighting process was confused by the Court's opinions concerning automobiles. He argued:

> From the several opinions that have been filed in this case it is apparent that the law of search and seizure is due for an overhauling. State and federal law enforcement officers and prosecutorial authorities must find quite intolerable the present state of uncertainty, which extends even to such an everyday question as the circumstances under which police may enter a man's property to arrest him and seize a vehicle believed to have been used during the commission of a crime.

While recognizing the confusion, Justice Harlan did not offer a solution. Justice White and the other dissenters believed that much of the confusion could be cleared up if the Court simply ruled that automobiles could be searched without a warrant no matter where they were found. The majority of the justices were not ready to accept such a simple solution.

In this case, the majority of justices may have believed that Edward Coolidge had been sentenced to life in prison on very slim evidence. The only way these justices found to right what they thought was an injustice in this particular case was to throw out the search of the car that provided the key evidence against him.

INVENTORY SEARCHES OF AUTOMOBILES

By 1973 Justices Rehnquist and Powell had been added to the Burger Court in part, many believed, to clear up some of the confusion in this area of search and seizure law. The law did become less confusing with the 1973 decision in *Cady v. Dombrowski*. The case concerned Chester J. Dombrowski, who was involved in an automobile accident in a small Wisconsin town. The police arrested him and towed his car to a garage, where they performed an inventory search of the car the next day. They found several items with blood on them that were ultimately used at Dombrowski's trial for a murder that was totally unrelated to the accident. Dombrowski was convicted of murder, and his attorney argued that the police should have gotten a warrant before searching his car.

The five-justice majority did not agree. Justice Rehnquist, in writing the majority opinion, argued that the police had every right to take the car into custody after the accident, and therefore they had every right to search the car without a search warrant. Dombrowski's conviction was upheld. Justices Brennan, Douglas, Stewart, and Marshall dissented, arguing that past decisions required the police to obtain a search warrant in this case.

In 1976 the Court again divided five to four over the warrantless search of an automobile in *South Dakota v. Opperman*, with Chief Justice Burger writing the opinion for the majority. In this case, Donald Opperman's car had been towed by the police because it was parked in a no-parking zone. It was routine procedure for this police department to conduct a search of every car brought into the police garage so the items in the car could be listed in an inventory. During this routine inventory search, the police found marijuana. Opperman was convicted of marijuana possession and served 14 days in jail. His attorney objected that the police did not have either probable cause or a warrant in this case.

Chief Justice Burger ruled that the police did not need either. It was reasonable for police to take a car into custody under the circumstances of this case and to conduct an inventory search both to protect the owner's property and to protect the police from any dangerous materials that might be in the car. Justice Powell wrote a concurring opinion in which he pointed out that the Court had not created a general "automobile exception" to the warrant requirement, just exceptions in certain circumstances, such as the circumstances in this case. Justices Marshall, Brennan, Stewart, and White dissented, arguing that the police should have either probable cause or a warrant to search a car under these circumstances.

SEARCHING BAGGAGE IN AUTOMOBILES

In the 1977 case of *United States v. Chadwick*, the U.S. Justice Department asked the Burger Court to clear up the confusion surrounding the Fourth Amendment by making a general rule that a warrant would only be required to search a building. The Justice Department argued that no warrant should be required for searches and seizures of other things, such as automobiles and luggage; only probable cause should be required. The majority of justices rejected this idea out of hand.

In *Chadwick* police in a Boston train station noticed two people carrying a heavy footlocker. The police had a trained dog sniff the footlocker and the dog confirmed that there was marijuana inside. Later, Joseph Chadwick met the two people and placed the footlocker in the trunk of his car. The police then arrested all three people and took the car, complete with footlocker, to the federal building. An hour and a half later, the footlocker was opened to reveal a large amount of marijuana.

Chief Justice Burger ruled that in this case the police should have gotten a search warrant before opening the footlocker. This footlocker was a private place and deserved the full protection of the Fourth Amendment. While the police had every right to seize the footlocker after the dog confirmed that marijuana was inside, they should not have opened it without a search warrant.

The chief justice was incensed at the Justice Department's suggestion that the Court should create a simple, straightforward rule stating that warrants would only be required for searches of buildings and probable cause would justify all other searches and seizures. From 1886 onward, the Court had stuck by one general principle in interpreting the Fourth Amendment: a warrant is required unless obtaining one is not practical. In this case it was clearly practical for the police to obtain a search warrant once they had seized the car and footlocker. Chief Justice Burger and the other seven justices in the majority were not willing to break with what they considered to be almost a century of Supreme Court rulings interpreting the Fourth Amendment. It did not seem to bother these justices that the police were allowed to seize something without a warrant but were then required to obtain a warrant before searching it.

In his dissenting opinion, Justice Blackmun, joined by Justice Rehnquist, argued that it was time for the Court to clear up some of the confusion about search and seizure and come up with a straightforward doctrine, at least where automobiles and baggage inside automobiles are concerned. In his opinion, the new rule should be that a warrant is "not required to seize and search any movable property in the possession of a person properly arrested in a public place." He thought that cars and footlockers should be treated the same, regardless of whether the footlocker happened to be either inside or outside of a car trunk. The police in this situation could not really leave the footlocker and arrest these people. If the police have the authority to seize the footlocker, he suggested, then they should also have the authority to search it. According to Justice Blackmun, nothing was really gained by making the police go through the process of getting a search warrant in these kinds of situations. He could not imagine that there would ever be a time when a judge faced with these facts would refuse to issue such a warrant. However, the Burger Court was not ready to make what it considered to be a clear break with past Court rulings in this area. Joseph Chadwick's conviction for possession of marijuana was overturned.

By 1981 a third justice, Justice Stevens, had joined justices Blackmun and Rehnquist in dissenting from the "automobile/luggage" rule, if it can be called that. The case was *Robbins v. California*. On January 5, 1975, police stopped Jeffrey Robbins's car because he had been driving erratically. After opening Robbins's car door and smelling marijuana smoke, the police searched Robbins and the inside of his car and found marijuana. They then arrested Robbins and searched the luggage compartment of the car. In doing so, they unwrapped two plastic packages, which also contained marijuana.

Justice Stewart, writing for the six-justice majority, ruled that the police had the authority to search the area around Robbins when they arrested him (as a search incident to an arrest, which allows police to search the person and the area under his immediate control), but they should have gotten a search warrant before searching the luggage compartment of his automobile. Robbins's conviction for possessing the large amount of marijuana found in the trunk was overturned, but his conviction for possessing the small amount of marijuana found inside the car was upheld.

Justice Blackmun's dissenting opinion once again pointed to the confusion that this and other decisions by the Court had caused for both the police and the citizens. He argued that the Court should lay down a simple, clear rule so that people would know when their rights were being violated without a legal opinion from an attorney and police would know when they did and did not need a search warrant.

Finally, by 1991, Justice Blackmun had convinced a majority of the other justices that confusion could only be eliminated if the Court handed down a simple, straightforward rule concerning automobiles and the things police find inside automobiles. Justice Blackmun wrote the opinion for the majority in *California v. Acevedo* (see p. 87). In this case police had probable cause to stop and search Charles Acevedo's automobile because they believed a paper bag inside the car contained marijuana. The question for the Court was whether the police needed a search warrant before they could search a closed paper bag they found inside the trunk.

Justice Blackmun ruled that they did not. Once the police had probable cause to either arrest Charles Acevedo or search his car or its contents, they did not need to get a warrant before searching the container they found inside the trunk. There would be a true "automobile exception" to the warrant requirement and it would include the trunk and any closed containers found either in the cab of the car or in the trunk.

Also, if police have probable cause to search a container that is located inside a car (such as the footlocker in the *Chadwick* case or the paper bag in this case) they may do so without first obtaining a search warrant. Justice Blackmun pointed out that since the police already have probable cause to seize the container inside the car forcing them to obtain a warrant did not really protect anyone. There would now be a simple rule concerning both automobiles and containers inside of automobiles: police with probable cause may search them in the field or back at the station. Police may search containers inside a car if they have probable cause to arrest the driver or if they have probable cause to believe there is something illegal inside the containers that are inside the car. With this decision, the technical and complex distinctions developed over two decades by the Warren and Burger Courts were abandoned. Justice Blackmun went on to say:

> Until today, this Court has drawn a curious line between the search of an automobile that coincidentally turns up a container and the search of a container that coincidentally turns up in an automobile. The protections of the Fourth Amendment must not turn on such coincidences. We therefore interpret *Carroll* as providing one rule to govern all automobile searches. The police may search an automobile and the containers within it where they have probable cause to believe contraband or evidence is contained.

Justices Stevens, Marshall, and White dissented, arguing that this was too great a departure from past precedent in this area.

Justice Scalia wrote a concurring opinion in which he urged the Court to go further. He argued:

> It is anomalous for a briefcase to be protected by a "general require-ment" of a prior warrant when it is being carried along the street, but for that same briefcase to become unprotected as soon as it is carried into an automobile. . . . Under these principles, if a known drug dealer is carrying a briefcase reasonably believed to contain marijuana (the unau-thorized possession of which is a crime), the police may arrest him and search his person on the basis of probable cause alone. And, under our precedents, upon arrival at the station house, the police may inventory his possessions, including the briefcase, even if there is no reason to suspect that they contain contraband. . . . According to our current law, however, the police may not, on the basis of the same probable cause, take the less intrusive step of stopping the individual on the street and demanding to see the contents of his briefcase. That makes no sense. . . . I would reverse the judgment in the present case, not because a closed container carried inside a car becomes subject to the "automobile excep-tion" to the general warrant requirement, but because the search of a closed container, outside a privately owned building, with probable cause to believe that the container contains contraband, and when it in fact does contain contraband, is not one of those searches whose Fourth Amendment reasonableness depends upon a warrant. For that reason I concur in the judgment of the Court.

While Justice Scalia is right that the new rule does seem a little strange, it is not confusing. Police do not need a warrant to search or seize an automo-bile, including everything inside that automobile. They do not need a warrant to search or seize a person, along with anything that person might be carrying, such as a footlocker or backpack, which may then be "inventory searched" at the police station, with one possible exception. If the police have seized the person *because* they believe the luggage he or she is carrying contains contraband or illegal drugs or evidence of a crime, they may have to take the person and the luggage to a judge and obtain a search warrant before opening it.

Justice Scalia, in his concurring opinion, suggested that police would be able to conduct an inventory search in this situation, but this statement is a classic example of what is called dicta. Justice Scalia was giving his personal opinion, but that personal opinion is not binding on future decisions, and it could be argued that in this case his personal opinion was an inaccurate statement of the law. It remains to be seen whether at some point in the future a majority of justices will remove the warrant requirement for searches of suspect baggage.

CONCLUSION

In 1925 in the *Carroll* case the Supreme Court began down a road that would ultimately lead to great confusion on the part of both the police and the public. The Court ruled that, in general, where practical, police would have to get a warrant before searching or seizing anyone or anything. At the same time, the unanimous Court ruled that in the case of automobiles this requirement was not practical or reasonable. Police would only be expected to have probable cause, not a warrant, before seizing and searching an automobile.

While seemingly clear, that decision left a lot of questions unanswered. Those unanswered questions led the Court to create and then abandon a series of "rules" concerned with the search and seizure of automobiles and their contents. Both the Warren and Burger Courts were befuddled by this problem. Finally the Rehnquist Court came up with a straightforward rule that both the police and the average citizen could understand. Police with probable cause may search and seize both automobiles and their contents, including locked footlockers in car trunks, even if the only reason for stopping the car is to search the locked footlocker. Whether or not the Court will rule in the future that police with probable cause may search a footlocker in a public place instead of having to seize it and then obtain a search warrant remains to be seen.

Looking back over three generations of decisions about automobiles and luggage, some people might question whether this trip was really necessary. Throughout the 1960s, 1970s, and 1980s police cried out for a set of simple guidelines from the Court. Wouldn't it have been better if the Court in 1925 had simply ruled that warrants are needed to search buildings and probable cause is needed to search or seize anything else, from footlockers in train stations to cars in driveways? Of course that would have been simpler, but that is not the way the Supreme Court operates. The Court is not a legislature; it can only take the cases that come before it. Also, if the Court had not experimented with a much broader warrant requirement, we would never have known that such a rule is impossible to interpret and enforce in the real world.

Rights that the average person and police officer cannot understand are not worth much. That is perhaps one of the major lessons the Supreme Court learned as it struggled to come up with reasonable rules for the search and seizure of automobiles and luggage.

.... CASE DECISIONS ....

Carroll v. United States involved the search of an automobile on the open road by federal agents looking for illegal liquor. A unanimous Supreme Court agreed that the Fourth Amendment did not require police to get a search warrant before searching an automobile on the open road. Government officials must, however, have probable cause to believe they will find something illegal or evidence of a crime before they may search an automobile. The majority opinion, by Chief Justice Taft, is included here. Justice McReynolds wrote a dissenting opinion in which he argued that the agents in this case did not have probable cause. His dissenting opinion is also included.

California v. Acevedo involved the issue of whether or not police may search containers found in automobiles without a search warrant. A majority of justices ruled that they may do so if they have probable cause. Justice Blackmun wrote the majority opinion, which is included here. Justice Scalia wrote a concurring opinion and Justice Stevens wrote a dissenting opinion, neither of which are included.

Following are excerpts from the case decisions.

❀ ❀ ❀ ❀ ❀ ❀ ❀ ❀

CARROLL v. UNITED STATES
267 U.S. 132 (1925)

MR. CHIEF JUSTICE TAFT . . . delivered the opinion of the Court. . . .

[T]he guaranty of freedom from unreasonable searches and seizures by the Fourth Amendment has been construed, practically since the beginning of the Government, as recognizing a necessary difference between a search of a store, dwelling house or other structure in respect of which a proper official warrant readily may be obtained, and a search of a ship, motor boat, wagon or automobile, for contraband goods, where it is not practicable to secure a warrant because the vehicle can be quickly moved out of the locality or jurisdiction in which the warrant must be sought.

Having thus established that contraband goods concealed and illegally transported in an automobile or other vehicle may be searched for without a warrant, we come now to consider under what circumstances such search may be made. It would be intolerable and unreasonable if a prohibition agent were authorized to stop every automobile on the chance of finding liquor and thus subject all persons lawfully using the highways to the inconvenience and indignity of such a search. Travellers may be so stopped in crossing an international boundary because of national self protection reasonably requiring one entering the country to identify himself as entitled to come in, and his belongings as effects which may be lawfully brought in. But those lawfully within the country, entitled to use the public highways, have a right to free passage without interruption or search unless there is known to a competent official authorized to search, probable cause for believing that their vehicles are carrying contraband or illegal merchandise. . . .

It follows from this that if an officer seizes an automobile or the liquor in it without a warrant and the facts as subsequently developed do not justify a judgment of condemnation and forfeiture, the officer may escape costs or a suit for damages by a showing that he had reasonable or probable cause for the seizure. *Stacey v. Emery*, 97 U.S. 642. The measure of legality of such a seizure is, therefore, that the seizing officer shall have reasonable or probable cause for believing that the automobile which he stops and seizes has contraband liquor therein which is being illegally transported.

We here find the line of distinction between legal and illegal seizures of liquor in transport in vehicles. It is certainly a reasonable distinction. It gives the owner of an automobile or other vehicle seized under Section 26, in absence of probable cause, a right to have restored to him the automobile, it protects him under the *Weeks* and *Amos* cases from use of the liquor as evidence against him, and it subjects the officer making the seizures to damages. On the other hand, in a case showing probable cause, the Government and its officials are given the opportunity which they should have, to make the investigation necessary to trace reasonably suspected contraband goods and to seize them.

Such a rule fulfills the guaranty of the Fourth Amendment. In cases where the securing of a warrant is reasonably practicable, it must be used, and when properly supported by affidavit and issued after judicial approval protects the seizing officer against a suit for damages. In cases where seizure is impossible except without warrant, the seizing officer acts unlawfully and at his peril unless he can show the court probable cause. . . .

Finally, was there probable cause? . . .

We know . . . that Grand Rapids is about 152 miles from Detroit and that Detroit and its neighborhood along the Detroit River, which is the International Boundary, is one of the most active centers for introducing illegally into this country spiritous liquors for distribution into the interior. It is obvious from the evidence that the prohibition agents were engaged in a regular patrol along the important highways from Detroit to Grand Rapids to stop and seize liquor carried in automobiles. They knew or had convincing evidence to make them believe that the Carroll boys, as they called them, were so-called "bootleggers" in Grand Rapids, i.e., that they were engaged in plying the unlawful trade of selling such liquor in that city. The officers had soon after noted their going from Grand Rapids half way to Detroit and attempted to follow them to that city to see where they went, but they escaped observation. Two months later these officers suddenly met the same men on their way westward presumably from Detroit. . . . They were coming from the direction of the great source of supply for their stock to Grand Rapids where they plied their trade. That the officers when they saw the defendants believed that they were carrying liquor we can have no doubt, and we think it is equally clear that they had reasonable cause for thinking so. Emphasis is put by defendants' counsel on the statement made by one of the officers that they were not looking for defendants at the particular time when they appeared. We do not perceive that it has any weight. As soon as they did appear, the officers were entitled to use their reasoning faculties upon all the facts of which they had previous knowledge in respect to the defendants. . . .

[I]t is clear the officers here had justification for the search and seizure. This is to say that the facts and circumstances within their knowledge and of which they had reasonably trustworthy information were sufficient in themselves to warrant a man of reasonable caution in the belief that intoxicating liquor was being transported in the automobile which they stopped and searched.

Dissenting Opinion The separate opinion of MR. JUSTICE MCREYNOLDS concurred in by MR. JUSTICE SUTHERLAND.

While quietly driving an ordinary automobile along a much frequented public road, plaintiffs in error were arrested by Federal officers without a warrant and upon mere suspicion—ill founded, as I think. The officers then searched the machine and discovered carefully secreted whisky, which was seized and thereafter used as evidence against plaintiffs in error when on trial for transporting intoxicating liquor contrary to the Volstead Act (c. 85, 41 Stat. 305). They maintain that both arrest and seizure were unlawful and that use of the liquor as evidence violated their constitutional rights. . . .

The facts known by the officers who arrested plaintiffs in error were wholly insufficient to create a reasonable belief that they were transporting liquor contrary to law. These facts were detailed by Fred Cronenwelt, chief prohibition officer. His . . . testimony as given at the trial follows—

"I am in charge of the Federal Prohibition Department in this District. I am acquainted with these two respondents, and first saw them on September 29, 1921, in Mr. Scully's apartment on Oakes Street, Grand Rapids. There

were three of them that came to Mr. Scully's apartment, one by the name of
Kruska, George Kiro and John Carroll. I was introduced to them under the
name of Stafford, and told them I was working for the Michigan Chair
Company, and wanted to buy three cases of whisky, and the price was agreed
upon. After they thought I was all right, they said they would be back in half
or three-quarters of an hour; that they had to go out to the east end of Grand
Rapids, to get this liquor. They went away and came back in a short time, and
Mr. Kruska came upstairs and said they couldn't get it that night; that a
fellow by the name of Irving, where they were going to get it, wasn't in, but
they were going to deliver it the next day, about ten. They didn't deliver it
the next day. I am not positive about the price. It seems to me it was around
$130 a case. It might be $135. Both respondents took part in this conversation. When they came to Mr. Scully's apartment they had this same car.
While it was dark and I wasn't able to get a good look at this car, later, on the
sixth day of October, when I was out on the road with Mr. Scully, I was
waiting on the highway while he went to Reed's Lake to get a light lunch,
and they drove by, and I had their license number and the appearance of
their car, and knowing the two boys, seeing them on the 29th day of
September, I was satisfied when I seen the car on December 15th it was the
same car I had seen on the 6th day of October. On the 6th day of October it
was probably twenty minutes before Scully got back to where I was. I told him
the Carroll boys had just gone toward Detroit and we were trying to catch up
with them and see where they were going. We did catch up with them
somewhere along by Ada, just before we got to Ada, and followed them to
East Lansing. We gave up the chase at East Lansing.

"On the 15th of December, when Peterson and Scully and I overhauled
this car on the road, it was in the country, on Pike 16, the road leading
between Grand Rapids and Detroit. When we passed the car we were going
toward Ionia, or Detroit, and the Kiro and Carroll boys were coming towards
Grand Rapids when Mr. Scully and I recognized them and said 'there goes the
Carroll brothers,' and we went on still further in the same direction we were
going and turned around and went back to them; drove up to the side of
them. Mr. Scully was driving the car; I was sitting in the front seat, and I
stepped out on the running board and held out my hand and said, 'Carroll,
stop that car,' and they did stop it. John Kiro was driving the car. After we got
them stopped, we asked them to get out of the car, which they did. Carroll
referred to me and called me by the name of 'Fred' just as soon as I got up to
him. Raised up the back part of the roadster; didn't find any liquor there;
then raised up the cushion; then I struck at the lazyback of the seat and it was
hard. I then started to open it up, and I did tear the cushion some, and Carroll
said, 'Don't tear the cushion; we have only got six cases in there;' and I took
out two bottles and found out it was liquor; satisfied it was liquor." . . .

The negotiation concerning three cases of whisky on September 29th was the only circumstance which could have subjected plaintiffs in error to any reasonable suspicion. No whisky was delivered, and it is not certain that they ever intended to deliver any. The arrest came two and a half months after the negotiation. Every act in the meantime is consistent with complete innocence. Has it come about that merely because a man once agreed to deliver whisky, but did not, he may be arrested whenever thereafter he ventures to drive an automobile on the road to Detroit!

CALIFORNIA v. ACEVEDO
111 S. Ct. 1982 (1991)

JUSTICE BLACKMUN delivered the opinion of the Court.

This case requires us once again to consider the so-called "automobile exception" to the warrant requirement of the Fourth Amendment and its application to the search of a closed container in the trunk of a car.

On October 28, 1987, Officer Coleman of the Santa Ana, Cal., Police Department received a telephone call from a federal drug enforcement agent in Hawaii. The agent informed Coleman that he had seized a package containing marijuana which was to have been delivered to the Federal Express Office in Santa Ana and which was addressed to J.R. Daza at 805 West Stevens Avenue in that city. The agent arranged to send the package to Coleman instead. Coleman then was to take the package to the Federal Express office and arrest the person who arrived to claim it.

Coleman received the package on October 29, verified its contents, and took it to the Senior Operations Manager at the Federal Express office. At about 10:30 A.M. on October 30, a man, who identified himself as Jamie Daza, arrived to claim the package. He accepted it and drove to his apartment on West Stevens. He carried the package into the apartment.

At 11:45 A.M., officers observed Daza leave the apartment and drop the box and paper that had contained the marijuana into a trash bin. Coleman at that point left the scene to get a search warrant. About 12:05 P.M., the officers saw Richard St. George leave the apartment carrying a blue knapsack which appeared to be half full. The officers stopped him as he was driving off, searched the knapsack, and found 1 1/2 pounds of marijuana.

At 12:30 P.M., respondent Charles Steven Acevedo arrived. He entered Daza's apartment, stayed for about 10 minutes, and reappeared carrying a brown paper bag that looked full. The officers noticed that the bag was the size of one of the wrapped marijuana packages sent from Hawaii. Acevedo walked to a silver Honda in the parking lot. He placed the bag in the trunk of the car and started to drive away. Fearing the loss of evidence, officers in a marked police car stopped him. They opened the trunk and the bag, and found marijuana.

Respondent was charged in state court with possession of marijuana for sale, in violation of Cal. Health & Safety Code Ann. § 11359 (West Supp. 1987). App. 2. He moved to suppress the marijuana found in the car. The motion was denied. He then pleaded guilty but appealed the denial of the suppression motion.

The California Court of Appeal, Fourth District, concluded that the marijuana found in the paper bag in the car's trunk should have been suppressed. *People v. Acevedo*, 216 Cal.App.3d. 586, 265 Cal.Rptr. 23 (1990). The court concluded that the officers had probable cause to believe that the paper bag contained drugs but lacked probable cause to suspect that Acevedo's car, itself, otherwise contained contraband. Because the officers' probable cause was directed specifically at the bag, the court held that the case was controlled by *United States v. Chadwick*, 433 U.S. 1, 97 S. Ct. 2476, 53 L.Ed.2d 538 (1977), rather than by *United States v. Ross*, 456 U.S. 798, 102 S. Ct. 2157, 72 L.Ed.2d 572 (1982). Although the court agreed that the officers could seize the paper bag, it held that, under *Chadwick*, they could not open the bag without first obtaining a warrant for that purpose. The court then recognized "the anomalous nature" of the dichotomy between the rule in *Chadwick* and the rule in *Ross*. 216 Cal.App.3d, at 592, 265 Cal.Rptr., at 27. That dichotomy dictates that if there is probable cause to search a car, then the entire car—including any closed container found therein—may be searched without a warrant, but if there is probable cause only as to a container in the car, the container may be held but not searched until a warrant is obtained. . . .

The Fourth Amendment protects the "right of the people to be secure in their persons, houses, papers, and effects, against unreasonable searches and seizures." Contemporaneously with the adoption of the Fourth Amendment, the First Congress, and, later, the Second and Fourth Congresses, distinguished between the need for a warrant to search for contraband concealed in "a dwelling house or similar place" and the need for a warrant to search for contraband concealed in a movable vessel. . . . In *Carroll*, this Court established an exception to the warrant requirement for moving vehicles, for it recognized

> "a necessary difference between a search of a store, dwelling house or other structure in respect of which a proper official warrant readily may be obtained, and a search of a ship, motor boat, wagon or automobile, for contraband goods, where it is not practicable to secure a warrant because the vehicle can be quickly moved out of the locality or jurisdiction in which the warrant must be sought." 267 U.S., at 153, 45 S. Ct., at 285.

It therefore held that a warrantless search of an automobile based upon probable cause to believe that the vehicle contained evidence of crime in the light of an exigency arising out of the likely disappearance of the vehicle did not contravene the Warrant Clause of the Fourth Amendment. See *id.*, at 158–159, 45 S. Ct., at 287.

The Court refined the exigency requirement in *Chambers v. Maroney*, 399 U.S. 42, 90 S. Ct. 1975, 26 L.Ed.2d 419 (1970), when it held that the existence of exigent circumstances was to be determined at the time the automobile is seized. The car search at issue in *Chambers* took place at the police station, where the vehicle was immobilized, some time after the driver had been arrested. Given probable cause and exigent circumstances at the time the vehicle was first stopped, the Court held that the later warrantless search at the station passed constitutional muster. The validity of the later search derived from the ruling in *Carroll* that an immediate search without a warrant at the moment of seizure would have been permissible. See *Chambers*, 399 U.S., at 51, 90 S. Ct., at 1981. The Court reasoned in *Chambers* that the police could search later whenever they could have searched earlier, had they so chosen. *Id.*, at 51–52, 90 S. Ct., at 1981. Following *Chambers*, if the police have probable cause to justify a warrantless seizure of an automobile on a public roadway, they may conduct either an immediate or a delayed search of the vehicle.

In *United States v. Ross*, 456 U.S. 798, 102 S. Ct. 2157, 72 L.Ed.2d 572, decided in 1982, we held that a warrantless search of an automobile under the *Carroll* doctrine could include a search of a container or package found inside the car when such a search was supported by probable cause. The warrantless search of Ross' car occurred after an informant told the police that he had seen Ross complete a drug transaction using drugs stored in the trunk of his car. The police stopped the car, searched it, and discovered in the trunk a brown paper bag containing drugs. We decided that the search of Ross' car was not unreasonable under the Fourth Amendment: "The scope of a warrantless search based on probable cause is no narrower—and no broader—than the scope of a search authorized by a warrant supported by probable cause." *Id.*, at 823, 102 S. Ct., at 2172. Thus, "[i]f probable cause justifies the search of a lawfully stopped vehicle, it justifies the search of every part of the vehicle and its contents that may conceal the object of the search." *Id.*, at 825, 102 S. Ct., at 2173. In *Ross*, therefore, we clarified the scope of the *Carroll* doctrine as properly including a "probing search" of compartments and containers within the automobile so long as the search is supported by probable cause. *Id.*, at 800, 102 S. Ct., at 2160.

In addition to this clarification, *Ross* distinguished the *Carroll* doctrine from the separate rule that governed the search of closed containers. See 456

U.S., at 817, 102 S. Ct., at 2169. The Court had announced this separate rule, unique to luggage and other closed packages, bags, and containers, in *United States v. Chadwick*, 433 U.S. 1, 97 S. Ct. 2476, 53 L.Ed.2d 538 (1977). In *Chadwick*, federal narcotics agents had probable cause to believe that a 200-pound double-locked footlocker contained marijuana. The agents tracked the locker as the defendants removed it from a train and carried it through the station to a waiting car. As soon as the defendants lifted the locker into the trunk of the car, the agents arrested them, seized the locker, and searched it. In this Court, the United States did not contend that the locker's brief contact with the automobile's trunk sufficed to make the *Carroll* doctrine applicable. Rather, the United States urged that the search of movable luggage could be considered analogous to the search of an automobile. 433 U.S., at 11–12, 97 S. Ct., at 2483–2484.

The Court rejected this argument because, it reasoned, a person expects more privacy in his luggage and personal effects than he does in his automobile. *Id.*, at 13, 97 S. Ct., at 2484. Moreover, it concluded that as "may often not be the case when automobiles are seized," secure storage facilities are usually available when the police seize luggage. *Id.*, at 13, n. 7, 97 S. Ct., at 2484, n. 7.

In *Arkansas v. Sanders*, 442 U.S. 753, 99 S. Ct. 2586, 61 L.Ed.2d 235 (1979), the Court extended *Chadwick*'s rule to apply to a suitcase actually being transported in the trunk of a car. In *Sanders*, the police had probable cause to believe a suitcase contained marijuana. They watched as the defendant placed the suitcase in the trunk of a taxi and was driven away. The police pursued the taxi for several blocks, stopped it, found the suitcase in the trunk, and searched it. Although the Court had applied the *Carroll* doctrine to searches of integral parts of the automobile itself, (indeed, in *Carroll*, contraband whiskey was in the upholstery of the seats, see 267 U.S., at 136, 45 S. Ct., at 281), it did not extend the doctrine to the warrantless search of personal luggage "merely because it was located in an automobile lawfully stopped by the police." 442 U.S., at 765, 99 S. Ct., at 2594. Again, the *Sanders* majority stressed the heightened privacy expectation in personal luggage and concluded that the presence of luggage in an automobile did not diminish the owner's expectation of privacy in his personal items. *Id.*, at 764–765, 99 S. Ct., at 2593–2594. Cf. *California v. Carney*, 471 U.S. 386, 105 S. Ct. 2066, 85 L.Ed.2d 406 (1985).

In *Ross*, the Court endeavored to distinguish between *Carroll*, which governed the *Ross* automobile search, and *Chadwick*, which governed the *Sanders* automobile search. It held that the *Carroll* doctrine covered searches of automobiles when the police had probable cause to search an entire vehicle but that the *Chadwick* doctrine governed searches of luggage when the officers had probable cause to search only a container within the vehicle.

Thus, in a *Ross* situation, the police could conduct a reasonable search under the Fourth Amendment without obtaining a warrant, whereas in a *Sanders* situation, the police had to obtain a warrant before they searched. . . .

The facts in this case closely resemble the facts in *Ross*. In *Ross*, the police had probable cause to believe that drugs were stored in the trunk of a particular car. See 456 U.S., at 800, 102 S. Ct., at 2160. Here, the California Court of Appeal concluded that the police had probable cause to believe that respondent was carrying marijuana in a bag in his car's trunk. 216 Cal.App.3d, at 590, 265 Cal.Rptr., at 25. Furthermore, for what it is worth, in *Ross*, as here, the drugs in the trunk were contained in a brown paper bag.

This Court in *Ross* rejected *Chadwick*'s distinction between containers and cars. It concluded that the expectation of privacy in one's vehicle is equal to one's expectation of privacy in the containers, and noted that "the privacy interests in a car's trunk or glove compartment may be no less than those in a movable container." 456 U.S., at 823, 102 S. Ct., at 2172. It also recognized that it was arguable that the same exigent circumstances that permit a warrantless search of an automobile would justify the warrantless search of a movable container. *Id.*, at 809, 102 S. Ct., at 2165. In deference to the rule of *Chadwick* and *Sanders*, however, the Court put that question to one side. *Id.*, at 809–810, 102 S. Ct., at 2165. It concluded that the time and expense of the warrant process would be misdirected if the police could search every cubic inch of an automobile until they discovered a paper sack, at which point the Fourth Amendment required them to take the sack to a magistrate for permission to look inside. We now must decide the question deferred in *Ross*: whether the Fourth Amendment requires the police to obtain a warrant to open the sack in a movable vehicle simply because they lack probable cause to search the entire car. We conclude that it does not.

Dissenters in *Ross* asked why the suitcase in *Sanders* was "more private, less difficult for police to seize and store, or in any other relevant respect more properly subject to the warrant requirement, than a container that police discover in a probable-cause search of an entire automobile?" *Id.*, 456 U.S., at 839–840, 102 S. Ct., at 2180–2181. We now agree that a container found after a general search of the automobile and a container found in a car after a limited search for the container are equally easy for the police to store and for the suspect to hide or destroy. In fact, we see no principled distinction in terms of either the privacy expectation or the exigent circumstances between the paper bag found by the police in *Ross* and the paper bag found by the police here. Furthermore, by attempting to distinguish between a container for which the police are specifically searching and a container which they come across in a car, we have provided only minimal protection for privacy and have impeded effective law enforcement.

The line between probable cause to search a vehicle and probable cause to search a package in that vehicle is not always clear, and separate rules that govern the two objects to be searched may enable the police to broaden their power to make warrantless searches and disserve privacy interests. We noted this in *Ross* in the context of a search of an entire vehicle. Recognizing that under *Carroll*, the "entire vehicle itself . . . could be searched without a warrant," we concluded that "prohibiting police from opening immediately a container in which the object of the search is most likely to be found and instead forcing them first to comb the entire vehicle would actually exacerbate the intrusion on privacy interests." 456 U.S., at 821, n. 28, 102 S. Ct., at 2171, n. 28. At the moment when officers stop an automobile, it may be less than clear whether they suspect with a high degree of certainty that the vehicle contains drugs in a bag or simply contains drugs. If the police know that they may open a bag only if they are actually searching the entire car, they may search more extensively than they otherwise would in order to establish the general probable cause required by *Ross*.

Such a situation is not far fetched. In *United States v. Johns*, 469 U.S. 478, 105 S. Ct. 881, 83 L.Ed.2d 890 (1985), customs agents saw two trucks drive to a private airstrip and approach two small planes. The agents drew near the trucks, smelled marijuana, and then saw in the backs of the trucks packages wrapped in a manner that marijuana smugglers customarily employed. The agents took the trucks to headquarters and searched the packages without a warrant. *Id.*, at 481, 105 S. Ct., at 883. Relying on *Chadwick*, the defendants argued that the search was unlawful. *Id.*, at 482, 105 S. Ct., at 884. The defendants contended that *Ross* was inapplicable because the agents lacked probable cause to search anything but the packages themselves and supported this contention by noting that a search of the entire vehicle never occurred. *Id.*, at 483, 105 S. Ct., at 884. We rejected that argument and found *Chadwick* and *Sanders* inapposite because the agents had probable cause to search the entire body of each truck, although they had chosen not to do so. *Id.*, at 482–483, 105 S. Ct., at 884. We cannot see the benefit of a rule that requires law enforcement officers to conduct a more intrusive search in order to justify a less intrusive one.

To the extent that the *Chadwick-Sanders* rule protects privacy, its protection is minimal. Law enforcement officers may seize a container and hold it until they obtain a search warrant. *Chadwick*, 433 U.S., at 13, 97 S. Ct., at 2484. "Since the police, by hypothesis, have probable cause to seize the property, we can assume that a warrant will be routinely forthcoming in the overwhelming majority of cases." *Sanders*, 442 U.S., at 770, 99 S. Ct., at 2596 (dissenting opinion). And the police often will be able to search containers without a warrant, despite the *Chadwick-Sanders* rule, as a search incident to a lawful arrest. . . .

Finally, the search of a paper bag intrudes far less on individual privacy than does the incursion sanctioned long ago in *Carroll*. In that case, prohibition agents slashed the upholstery of the automobile. This Court nonetheless found their search to be reasonable under the Fourth Amendment. If destroying the interior of an automobile is not unreasonable, we cannot conclude that looking inside a closed container is. In light of the minimal protection to privacy afforded by the *Chadwick-Sanders* rule, and our serious doubt whether that rule substantially serves privacy interests, we now hold that the Fourth Amendment does not compel separate treatment for an automobile search that extends only to a container within the vehicle.

The *Chadwick-Sanders* rule not only has failed to protect privacy but it has also confused courts and police officers and impeded effective law enforcement. The conflict between the *Carroll* doctrine cases and the *Chadwick-Sanders* line has been criticized in academic commentary. . . .

The discrepancy between the two rules has led to confusion for law enforcement officers. For example, when an officer, who has developed probable cause to believe that a vehicle contains drugs, begins to search the vehicle and immediately discovers a closed container, which rule applies? The defendant will argue that the fact that the officer first chose to search the container indicates that his probable cause extended only to the container and that *Chadwick* and *Sanders* therefore require a warrant. On the other hand, the fact that the officer first chose to search in the most obvious location should not restrict the propriety of the search. The *Chadwick* rule, as applied to *Sanders*, has devolved into an anomaly such that the more likely the police are to discover drugs in a container, the less authority they have to search it. We have noted the virtue of providing " ' "clear and unequivocal" guidelines to the law enforcement profession.' ". . .

Although we have recognized firmly that the doctrine of *stare decisis* serves profoundly important purposes in our legal system, this Court has overruled a prior case on the comparatively rare occasion when it has bred confusion or been a derelict or led to anomalous results. See, *e.g.*, *Complete Auto Transit, Inc. v. Brady*, 430 U.S. 274, 288–289, 97 S. Ct. 1076, 1084, 51 L.Ed.2d 326 (1977). *Sanders* was explicitly undermined in *Ross*, 456 U.S., at 824, 102 S. Ct., at 2172, and the existence of the dual regimes for automobile searches that uncover containers has proved as confusing as the *Chadwick* and *Sanders* dissenters predicted. We conclude that it is better to adopt one clear-cut rule to govern automobile searches and eliminate the warrant requirement for closed containers set forth in *Sanders*.

The interpretation of the *Carroll* doctrine set forth in *Ross* now applies to all searches of containers found in an automobile. In other words, the police may search without a warrant if their search is supported by probable cause. The Court in *Ross* put it this way:

> "The scope of a warrantless search of an automobile . . . is not defined by the nature of the container in which the contraband is secreted. Rather, it is defined by the object of the search and the places in which there is probable cause to believe that it may be found." 456 U.S., at 824, 102 S. Ct., at 2172.

It went on to note: "Probable cause to believe that a container placed in the trunk of a taxi contains contraband or evidence does not justify a search of the entire cab." *Ibid.* We reaffirm that principle. In the case before us, the police had probable cause to believe that the paper bag in the automobile's trunk contained marijuana. That probable cause now allows a warrantless search of the paper bag. The facts in the record reveal that the police did not have probable cause to believe that contraband was hidden in any other part of the automobile and a search of the entire vehicle would have been without probable cause and unreasonable under the Fourth Amendment.

Our holding today neither extends the *Carroll* doctrine nor broadens the scope of the permissible automobile search delineated in *Carroll*, *Chambers*, and *Ross*. It remains a "cardinal principle that 'searches conducted outside the judicial process, without prior approval by judge or magistrate, are *per se* unreasonable under the Fourth Amendment—subject only to a few specifically established and well-delineated exceptions.' " *Mincey v. Arizona*, 437 U.S. 385, 390, 98 S. Ct. 2408, 2412, 57 L.Ed.2d 290 (1978), quoting *Katz v. United States*, 398 U.S. 347, 357, 88 S. Ct. 507, 514, 19 L.Ed.2d 576 (1967) (footnote omitted). We held in *Ross*: "The exception recognized in *Carroll* is unquestionably one that is 'specifically established and well delineated.' " 456 U.S., at 825, 102 S. Ct., at 514.

Until today, this Court has drawn a curious line between the search of an automobile that coincidentally turns up a container and the search of a container that coincidentally turns up in an automobile. The protections of the Fourth Amendment must not turn on such coincidences. We therefore interpret *Carroll* as providing one rule to govern all automobile searches. The police may search an automobile and the containers within it where they have probable cause to believe contraband or evidence is contained.

The judgment of the California Court of Appeal is reversed and the case is remanded to that court for further proceedings not inconsistent with this opinion.

It is so ordered.

....................................DISCUSSION QUESTIONS....................................

1. Over the years the Court has clearly changed its mind about what constitutes probable cause. In what way? Do you agree with the Court's change of mind?

2. If the Court had ruled that automobiles are simply not protected by the Fourth Amendment, how might the lives of average citizens be different?

3. The Court has struggled with deciding when police need a warrant before they may search an automobile. What is the current rule in this area? Do you agree with the Court that this is the only practical way to deal with this issue?

4. The Court has ruled that police may search baggage in an automobile without a warrant but may not search baggage outside of an automobile without a warrant. Do you think the Court is likely to change its mind on this issue in the near future?

5. In the *Chadwick* case, the U.S. Justice Department asked the Supreme Court to rule that warrants are only required to enter private buildings and that probable cause will justify the search or seizure of anything else anywhere else. Seven members of the Burger Court rejected this idea out of hand, including the chief justice. Do you think the current Court would be more receptive to this idea?

CHAPTER
six
❋ ❋ ❋ ❋ ❋ ❋ ❋ ❋ ❋

The Exclusionary Rule

.... **DISCUSSION** ....

The constitutional rules that surround the Fourth Amendment are unique. In many cases involving the Bill of Rights, the Court is faced with people who have been prosecuted because they wanted to exercise their constitutional rights. For example, the defendant might be someone who has relied on the right of free speech to make a speech in a public park. In most of these cases, the question for the Court is whether or not the person's actions were protected by the Constitution. If they were, then the person goes free. If they were not, then the person goes to jail. When the Fourth Amendment is involved, however, the situation is very different.

In most cases involving the Fourth Amendment, the defendants have not been prosecuted because they chose to exercise their constitutional rights. Far from it. Instead, the defendants in Fourth Amendment cases are usually people who have violated a section of the criminal code that everyone agrees the state has every right to enforce. For example, the defendants might be convicted murderers, drug smugglers, or robbers.

In Fourth Amendment cases, the police have violated a defendant's rights in the process of arresting him or her. In some of these cases, the police have simply made a constitutional mistake; they could have followed the rules and gotten the necessary evidence without violating anyone's rights. In other cases, however, the Supreme Court is faced with criminals who never would have been caught if the police had not violated the Fourth Amendment.

In addressing the difficult question of what to do when the Fourth Amendment has been violated, the Supreme Court has tried many approaches. The only one that actually seems to have worked is for the Court to apply what has come to be called the "exclusionary rule." The exclusionary rule simply says that if the police have obtained evidence in a way that violates the Fourth Amendment rights of the accused then that evidence must be excluded from the trial. If the trial judge did not exclude the evidence from the trial, then the Supreme Court must overturn the conviction. In some cases, the accused will be retried without the use of the illegally obtained evidence. In other cases, there will not be a retrial because the illegally obtained evidence was the basis of the prosecution's case. The story of the birth and evolution of the exclusionary rule is complex and demonstrates the unique problems the Supreme Court has had to face when interpreting the Fourth Amendment.

INVENTING THE EXCLUSIONARY RULE

The exclusionary rule was born in 1914 with very little fanfare and no dissent. In the case of *Weeks v. United States*, Fremont Weeks was convicted of selling lottery tickets through the mail, a federal offense. Without bothering to get a search warrant, federal agents entered and searched Weeks's home and seized documents and papers there. Some of these were used as evidence to convict Weeks. That was, in the eyes of the justices, a very clear violation of the Fourth Amendment. Before the trial began, Weeks's attorney asked the trial judge to return Weeks's property to him because it had been seized in violation of the Fourth Amendment, but the trial judge refused.

Writing the opinion for the unanimous Court, Justice Day focused specifically on the facts of this particular case. The search did not occur while Weeks was being arrested. Justice Day said:

> The case . . . involves the right of the court in a criminal prosecution to retain for the purposes of evidence the letters and correspondence of the accused, seized in his house in his absence and without his authority, by a United States Marshall holding no warrant for his arrest and none for the search of his premises. The accused, without awaiting his trial, made timely application to the court for an order for the return of these letters, as well as other property.

The Court emphasized that this was not a case of a defendant objecting to evidence at the point at which the prosecution wished to introduce it at trial. Instead, the accused had pointed out the constitutional problem to the judge before the trial, and the judge had refused to order the property returned.

The Court also made much of the fact that this property belonged to Weeks. The papers and documents were not stolen property or tools used in committing a crime; they were the defendant's property in the same way the invoice in the *Boyd* case, decided in 1886, was the property of the glass merchants. Justice Day went on to say:

> If letters and private documents can thus be seized and held and used in evidence against a citizen accused of an offense, the protection of the Fourth Amendment declaring his right to be secure against such searches and seizures is of no value, and, so far as those thus placed are concerned, might as well be stricken from the Constitution. The efforts of the courts and their officials to bring the guilty to punishment, praiseworthy as they are, are not to be aided by the sacrifice of those great principles established by years of endeavor and suffering which have resulted in their embodiment in the fundamental law of the land.

The U.S. attorney representing the prosecution noted that in past decisions the Supreme Court had accepted the argument that evidence introduced at trial may not be objected to because of the manner in which it had been obtained. These past rulings seemed to contradict the ruling in this case. Justice Day pointed out that there was no real contradiction. Those earlier decisions were based on the proposition that once a trial has begun the trial should not be sidetracked by issues such as the legality of the seizure of evidence. At that point, the issue would only serve to disrupt the orderly progress of the trial. In this case, however, Weeks's attorney had raised the issue before the trial and asked that the property be returned. Fremont Weeks's conviction was overturned.

In the *Weeks* case, the Court could not see that it had any real choice. What other remedy could it apply short of excluding the evidence from the trial? If the defendant went to prison based on evidence obtained in violation of his constitutional rights, what could the Court do to correct the violation? In other cases when people had been put in jail in violation of their constitutional rights the Court had ordered them released. Why should this case be different simply because it involved the Fourth Amendment?

In the 1925 case of *Agnello v. United States* (see p. 44), another unanimous Court affirmed the use of the exclusionary rule. Federal agents had searched Frank Agnello's room without a warrant, found illegal drugs there, and then introduced the drugs as evidence at his trial. Agnello was convicted of conspiracy to sell cocaine without paying the federal drug taxes. The Court ruled that Agnello's right to property and privacy had been violated because the agents acted without a warrant.

The U.S. attorney argued that the situation in the *Agnello* case was different from that in the *Weeks* case. A can of cocaine is different from private papers, and Agnello's attorney did not object to the introduction of this evidence until after the trial had begun. Justice Butler, writing for the unanimous Court, ruled that these differences from the facts in the *Weeks* case did not matter. Evidence obtained in violation of the Fourth Amendment could not be admitted if objected to, even if the objection was made during the trial and even if the item was contraband rather than the personal property of the defendant. In this case, Agnello argued that the can of cocaine was not his and therefore should not have been introduced as evidence at his trial. Justice Butler thought that it was unreasonable to expect Agnello's attorney to request the return of the can before the trial because Agnello claimed that the can was not his and because until the trial began the attorney did not know that the can would be introduced as evidence against his client. Justice Butler believed that a rule of procedure "must not be allowed for any technical reason to prevail over a constitutional right." Agnello's conviction was overturned.

EXTENDING THE EXCLUSIONARY RULE TO THE STATES

Both the *Weeks* and *Agnello* cases involved people charged with violating federal law. Early in the nineteenth century, the Supreme Court determined that the Bill of Rights only applied to the actions of the federal government. After the Civil War, the Fourteenth Amendment was passed, guaranteeing that every citizen in the United States would enjoy "liberty." What did that mean? Between the Civil War and the Great Depression, the Supreme Court decided that the Fourteenth Amendment protected some basic liberties from violation by the states, but the Court was not very specific about what those liberties were. Finally, beginning in the 1930s, the Court decided that the Fourteenth Amendment made the provisions of the Bill of Rights applicable to the states as well as the federal government. In 1949, in the case of *Wolf v. Colorado*, the Court came to the conclusion that the Fourteenth Amendment made the Fourth Amendment applicable to the states.

The difficult question for the Court was whether or not the exclusionary rule also applied to the states. Justice Frankfurter, writing for the six-justice majority, ruled that while the Fourth Amendment applied to the states the exclusionary rule did not.

Justice Frankfurter did find "the security of one's privacy against arbitrary intrusion by the police" to be the "core of the Fourth Amendment" and "basic to a free society." Therefore, this basic right would be considered part of the due process of law required by the Fourteenth Amendment. He went on to say that "the ways of enforcing such a basic right raise questions of a different order." What should the remedy for violating the Fourth Amendment be if evidence seized illegally could not be excluded from trials?

He noted that "most of the English-speaking world does not regard as vital to such protection the exclusion of evidence" obtained in violation of similar rights. Justice Frankfurter suggested that people whose rights had been violated could sue the people who had violated their rights and that public opinion would see to it that police were disciplined for violating the Fourth Amendment. While the majority of justices held that the Fourth Amendment applied to state and local governments, Wolf's conviction, which was obtained with the use of unconstitutionally seized evidence, was not overturned because the Court ruled that the exclusionary rule did not apply to state and local governments.

Justices Douglas, Murphy, and Rutledge dissented. Justice Murphy argued that realistically there are only three possible remedies when the Fourth Amendment has been violated by police: "judicial exclusion of the illegally obtained evidence; criminal prosecution of violators; and civil action against violators in the action of trespass." He then pointed out that two of these remedies are really an illusion. He said:

> But what an illusory remedy this is, if by 'remedy' we mean a positive deterrent to police and prosecutors tempted to violate the Fourth Amendment. The appealing ring softens when we recall that in a trespass action the measure of damages is simply the extent of the injury to physical property. If the officer searches with care, he can avoid all but nominal damages—a penny, or a dollar."

In other words, Murphy argued, police are not going to be put in jail for violating the Fourth Amendment, and if they are sued they are not going to have real judgments levied against them. To Justice Murphy and the other two dissenting justices, it was clear in 1949 that there was only one real remedy for a violation of the Fourth Amendment: the application of the exclusionary rule at the trial of the accused.

Justice Murphy also reviewed the police procedures in states that had imposed their own exclusionary rule, such as Texas, and found police officers trained in the rules of proper search and seizure. In New York, which had no exclusionary rule, police received no such training. He argued that the difference in training was a reflection of the efficacy of the exclusionary rule.

By 1961, with the decision in *Mapp v. Ohio* (see p. 107), a majority of justices had come to agree with the three dissenting justices in the *Wolf* case.

Dollree Mapp had been convicted of possessing "lascivious books and pictures" in violation of the Ohio obscenity laws, but the way in which the evidence had been obtained bothered the majority of justices. On May 23, 1957, Cleveland police officers knocked at the door of the Mapp house demanding entrance. Dollree Mapp called her attorney and then refused to admit the police without a warrant. Several hours later the police knocked again but no one answered. They then forced open the door and searched the house. The police believed that a "person wanted for questioning" in a recent bombing case might be hiding in the Mapp home.

When Dollree Mapp confronted the police and demanded to see a warrant, a police officer waved a piece of paper under her nose. Dollree Mapp grabbed the paper and stuffed it into her bra. The police then "recovered the piece of paper," handcuffed Dollree Mapp, and proceeded to search the house not just for a person, but for anything they could find, apparently taking revenge on Mapp because she had the audacity to insist on her constitutional rights. The search ultimately turned up some "obscene material," and Mapp was convicted for the possession of this material.

Justice Clark, who wrote the majority opinion in *Mapp v. Ohio*, traced the development of the Court's interpretation of the Fourth Amendment and the exclusionary rule, going back to the 1886 decision in *Boyd v. United States* and the 1914 decision in *Weeks v. United States*. He then reviewed the reasons the majority had given in *Wolf v. Colorado* for not making the exclusionary rule applicable to the states at the same time it made the Fourth Amendment applicable to the states. He found that in states without an exclusionary rule of their own "other remedies have been worthless and futile." As Justice Murphy had argued in *Wolf*, the exclusionary rule had proved to be the only effective way of enforcing the right to privacy and property protected by the Fourth Amendment. Mapp's conviction for the possession of obscene material was overturned because the evidence used against her had been obtained in violation of the Fourth Amendment and should have been excluded from her trial.

Justices Harlan, Frankfurter, and Whittaker dissented. Justice Harlan argued that this was not the appropriate case to overrule the exclusionary rule because the basis of the case's appeal to the Court was that the Ohio obscenity laws violated the right of free speech. He thought the majority had simply "reached out" to overrule *Wolf* without a proper foundation. Presumably the majority believed the facts of this case were so outrageous it was time to act rather than wait for years while other people endured similar outrageous violations of their Fourth Amendment rights.

THE LIMITS OF THE EXCLUSIONARY RULE

Needless to say, the *Mapp* decision on June 19, 1961, exploded like a bomb in the press, prompting stories of hundreds of murderers, rapists, and robbers who "got off" because of a "legal technicality." The press's criticism seemed contradictory, because in some cases the press criticized the police, often federal agents, for bursting into the homes of peaceful, law-abiding citizens, searching and terrorizing the residents, only to find that their "informants" had been wrong and the residents were not criminals after all. Because such people were never charged with any crime, the exclusionary rule did not provide them with any remedy for the violation of their constitutional rights. In 1971 the Supreme Court moved to provide such people with a remedy.

The case of *Bivens v. Six Unknown Agents* involved just such a raid. Without a search warrant, agents of the Federal Bureau of Narcotics burst into Webster Bivens's home, manacled Bivens in front of his wife and children, and then searched his apartment for drugs. Bivens was then taken to the federal courthouse in Brooklyn where he was interrogated, booked, and strip-searched. Bivens sued for $15,000 to compensate him for the mental suffering that had resulted from this unconstitutional behavior. Justice Brennan, writing the majority opinion, ruled that people who have had their rights violated by agents of the federal government may sue those agents and the federal government directly under the authority of the Bill of Rights.

Chief Justice Burger and Justices Black and Blackmun dissented, and each wrote a dissenting opinion. In his dissent, Chief Justice Burger discussed the shortcomings of the exclusionary rule and argued that it was up to Congress to deal with this problem, not the Supreme Court. He outlined the justifications that had been given for the exclusionary rule. First, the major justification seemed to be to deter unconstitutional conduct on the part of the police. If police know evidence will not be admitted if they violate the Constitution, they will follow the right procedure, assuming they know what the right procedure is. Second, government should not be allowed to profit from illegal acts. Third, people should not be asked to help in their own prosecution.

For Chief Justice Burger, the major argument in favor of the exclusionary rule was the "deterrent rationale—the hope that law enforcement officials would be deterred from unlawful searches and seizures if the illegally seized, albeit trustworthy, evidence was suppressed." In his opinion, the actions of the federal narcotics agents in the *Bivens* case demonstrated that the exclusionary rule was not having the desired deterrent effect. While he did not propose an alternative to the exclusionary rule, he did express the hope that some "meaningful substitute" could be developed. He also voiced his displeasure with the fact that what he considered minor violations of the dictates of the Fourth Amendment resulted in the same exclusion of evidence as flagrant violations. He argued that such a total all or nothing sanction as the exclusionary rule violated the principle that the punishment should fit the crime.

SEARCH WARRANTS AND THE EXCLUSIONARY RULE

In 1984, a majority of the justices reached a fundamental decision about the purpose and scope of the exclusionary rule. The case of *United States v. Leon* (see p. 110) involved a drug investigation by the Burbank, California, police department. The officers involved in the investigation prepared an affidavit, which was reviewed by several deputy district attorneys and then submitted to a judge, who issued a search warrant based on the affidavit. Homes were searched using the warrant and a large quantity of drugs was seized. The trial judge then threw out much of this evidence because in his opinion the affidavit did not meet the standards laid out by the U.S. Supreme Court in a number of decisions.

Justice White wrote the opinion for the majority. He ruled that the primary purpose of the exclusionary rule is to deter police from violating people's constitutional rights. The rule is supposed to encourage police to follow the dictates of the Fourth Amendment. The police in this case did just that; they obtained a search warrant signed by a judge and then proceeded to search. Nevertheless, they were still being punished because the judge who issued the warrant might not have had enough information to determine probable cause. Society was also being punished in this case because drug dealers would go free as a result.

Justice White believed the proper approach in this case was to weigh the "costs and benefits" of preventing this evidence from being used. The cost of excluding the evidence was obvious; criminals would now be free to commit more crimes. What was the benefit? The police had done everything the Supreme Court had asked them to do. They had prepared an affidavit stating why they wished to conduct the searches, and the judge who issued the warrant was satisfied that these searches would not be unreasonable given those circumstances. What benefit did society gain from throwing out this warrant and allowing these criminals to go free?

Justice White then ruled that as a general rule evidence will not be excluded if police obtain a search warrant before making a search, and that in most cases the Supreme Court will not examine the contents of the affidavit used to acquire the warrant or other technical aspects of the warrant procedure. The exclusionary rule would still apply, however, if the police know-ingly lied in their affidavit or showed a reckless disregard for the truth. Also, the exclusionary rule would still apply if the magistrate issuing the warrant was clearly not fulfilling the role of a "neutral and detached" protector of the public's right to privacy. Police would be expected to know whether the magistrate was doing this job. Also, a warrant could still be found to be clearly in violation of the Fourth Amendment, such as when it does not state the place to be searched or the things to be seized. Of course, police would still be expected to have probable cause in situations where a warrant is not required.

Justice White summarized his conclusion by saying:

> In the absence of an allegation that the magistrate abandoned his de-tached and neutral role, suppression is appropriate only if the officers were dishonest or reckless in preparing their affidavit or could not have harbored an objectively reasonable belief in the existence of probable cause.

There would now be a trial and the drugs seized could be used as evidence.

Justices Brennan, Marshall, and Stevens dissented. Justice Brennan ob-jected to what he saw as the "gradual but determined strangulation" of the exclusionary rule by the Burger Court. He did not find Justice White's evaluation of the costs and benefits convincing. Instead, he thought that the costs had been raised to "exaggerated heights" while the benefits had been "made to disappear with a mere wave of the hand." Justice Brennan argued that the exclusionary rule serves purposes other than just deterring illegal police conduct. It serves to limit the reach of the government into people's private lives. The fact that some evidence will be denied to the state is the obvious consequence of the Fourth Amendment and should not be used to justify limiting its power.

Justice Stevens put the problem this way:

> The Court assumes that the searches in these cases violated the Fourth Amendment, yet refuses to apply the exclusionary rule because the Court concludes that it was "reasonable" for the police to conduct them. In my opinion an official search and seizure cannot be both "unreasonable" and "reasonable" at the same time.

He went on to say that the Fourth Amendment specifically requires that a warrant be based on probable cause. If a warrant that is not based on probable cause can justify a search, then what is left of the Fourth Amendment? Justice Stevens also pointed to the other justification for the Fourth Amendment, that the integrity of the judicial process should be maintained.

There was another consideration that went unspoken by any of the justices in this decision but clearly weighed heavily on their minds. It was easy for a police officer who was willing to lie to write an affidavit that was assured of being acceptable. All of the Court's various tests could be met if the police officer made up a story. The officer could state that a "reliable" informant provided information that Mr. X had drugs in his house and that the informant based this information on his personal observation of the drugs in Mr. X's house. In other words, a well-written but fictional affidavit was beyond attack. It was only when the police officer told the truth and the judge who issued the warrant made a mistake that the evidence was excluded.

Justice White probably thought that the Court had two realistic choices: it could continue on the current course and find more and more fiction coming from the police, fiction that would be almost impossible to disprove, or it could take a different approach. Justice White and the majority decided to take a different approach.

THE HONEST MISTAKE EXCEPTION TO THE EXCLUSIONARY RULE

In 1990 the Court created another exception to the exclusionary rule. The case of *Illinois v. Rodriguez* involved the illegal search of an apartment. Police received consent to search Edward Rodriguez's apartment from a woman who had a key to the apartment and who the police believed in good faith was living in the apartment at the time. As it turned out, the woman was a "former" girlfriend of Edward Rodriguez and did not really have any authority to give the police permission to search his apartment. Based on evidence obtained from this search, Edward Rodriguez was convicted of possessing illegal drugs.

Justice Scalia wrote the opinion for the majority. Following the same logic as that used in the *Leon* case, Justice Scalia could not see how the purposes of the Fourth Amendment would be served by excluding the drugs found in Rodriguez's apartment. All the Fourth Amendment requires is that police act "reasonably," and Justice Scalia believed the police had acted reasonably, although erroneously, in this case. Edward Rodriguez's conviction was upheld.

Justices Marshall, Brennan, and Stevens dissented. Justice Marshall in his dissenting opinion argued that the majority had misunderstood past decisions, which had allowed anyone who lived in a home to consent to a search of that home. These decisions were not based on the idea that it is "reasonable" to allow other people to consent to a search but were instead based on the idea that "a person may voluntarily limit his expectation of privacy by allowing others to exercise authority over his possessions." In this case Edward Rodriguez had not done that. His privacy rights in his home were violated without a warrant and without his having given up those rights to the third party in question. In Justice Marshall's opinion this clearly should be seen as a violation of the Fourth Amendment.

CONCLUSION

Throughout the twentieth century the Supreme Court has found it impossible to enforce the dictates of the Fourth Amendment without using the exclusionary rule. At the same time, it has found the results of this rule, that the guilty may go free, to be difficult to live with. The Court has also had to accept the realities of modern law enforcement. For example, if police were required to name informants in affidavits or in court, there would be no more informants. But if police do not have to reveal the names of informants, how can the judicial system realistically verify what the police say the informant said? There is no easy answer. The Court has tried to develop a set of rules that it believes serve the fundamental purposes of the Fourth Amendment without unduly burdening the legitimate needs of law enforcement.

....CASE DECISIONS..

Mapp v. Ohio concerns whether or not the exclusionary rule should apply to the states. A majority of justices ruled that it did and overruled *Wolf v. Colorado* to the extent that it held otherwise. Justice Clark wrote the majority opinion, which is included here. Justices Black and Douglas wrote concurring opinions and Justice Harlan wrote a dissenting opinion, none of which are included.

In *United States v. Leon*, police conducted searches armed with search warrants and then found the evidence excluded from trial because the trial judge did not believe these warrants were based on probable cause. A majority of the justices ruled that police in most cases should be able to rely on a warrant issued by a detached and neutral magistrate. Justice White wrote the majority opinion, which is included here. Justices Blackmun, Brennan, and Stevens wrote dissenting opinions, which are not included.

Following are excerpts from the case decisions.

❋ ❋ ❋ ❋ ❋ ❋ ❋ ❋ ❋

MAPP v. OHIO
367 U.S. 643 (1961)

MR. JUSTICE CLARK delivered the opinion of the Court.

Appellant stands convicted of knowingly having had in her possession and under her control certain lewd and lascivious books, pictures, and photographs in violation of § 2905.34 of Ohio's Revised Code. As officially stated in the syllabus to its opinion, the Supreme Court of Ohio found that her conviction was valid though "based primarily upon the introduction in evidence of lewd and lascivious books and pictures unlawfully seized during an unlawful search of defendant's home. . . ." 170 Ohio St. 427–428, 166 N. E. 2d 387, 388.

On May 23, 1957, three Cleveland police officers arrived at appellant's residence in that city pursuant to information that "a person [was] hiding out in the home, who was wanted for questioning in connection with a recent bombing, and that there was a large amount of policy paraphernalia being hidden in the home." Miss Mapp and her daughter by a former marriage lived on the top floor of the two-family dwelling. Upon their arrival at that house, the officers knocked on the door and demanded entrance but appellant, after telephoning her attorney, refused to admit them without a search warrant. They advised their headquarters of the situation and undertook a surveillance of the house.

The officers again sought entrance some three hours later when four or more additional officers arrived on the scene. When Miss Mapp did not come to the door immediately, at least one of the several doors to the house was forcibly opened and the policemen gained admittance. Meanwhile Miss Mapp's attorney arrived, but the officers, having secured their own entry, and continuing in their defiance of the law, would permit him neither to see Miss Mapp nor to enter the house. It appears that Miss Mapp was halfway down the stairs from the upper floor to the front door when the officers, in this highhanded manner, broke into the hall. She demanded to see the search warrant. A paper, claimed to be a warrant, was held up by one of the officers. She grabbed the "warrant" and placed it in her bosom. A struggle ensued in which the officers recovered the piece of paper and as a result of which they handcuffed appellant because she had been "belligerent" in resisting their official rescue of the "warrant" from her person. Running roughshod over appellant, a policeman "grabbed" her, "twisted [her] hand," and she "yelled [and] pleaded with him" because "it was hurting." Appellant, in handcuffs, was then forcibly taken upstairs to her bedroom where the officers searched a dresser, a chest of drawers, a closet and some suitcases. They also looked into a photo album and through personal papers belonging to the appellant. The search spread to the rest of the second floor including the child's bedroom, the living room, the kitchen and a dinette. The basement of the building and a trunk found therein were also searched. The obscene materials for possession of which she was ultimately convicted were discovered in the course of that widespread search.

At the trial no search warrant was produced by the prosecution, nor was the failure to produce one explained or accounted for. At best, "There is, in the record, considerable doubt as to whether there ever was any warrant for the search of defendant's home." 170 Ohio St., at 430, 166 N. E. 2d, at 389. The Ohio Supreme Court believed a "reasonable argument" could be made that the conviction should be reversed "because the 'methods' employed to obtain the [evidence] . . . were such as to 'offend "a sense of justice," ' " but the court found determinative the fact that the evidence had not been taken "from defendant's person by the use of brutal or offensive physical force against defendant." 170 Ohio St., at 431, 166 N. E. 2d, at 389–390.

The State says that even if the search were made without authority, or otherwise unreasonably, it is not prevented from using unconstitutionally seized evidence at trial, citing *Wolf v. Colorado*, 338 U.S. 25 (1949), in which this Court did indeed hold "that in a prosecution in a State court for a State crime the Fourteenth Amendment does not forbid the admission of evidence obtained by an unreasonable search and seizure." At p. 33. On this appeal, of which we have noted probable jurisdiction, 364 U.S. 868, it is urged once again that we review that holding. . . .

In 1949, 35 years after *Weeks* was announced, this Court, in *Wolf v. Colorado, supra*, again for the first time, discussed the effect of the Fourth Amendment upon the States through the operation of the Due Process Clause of the Fourteenth Amendment. It said:

> "[W]e have no hesitation in saying that were a State affirmatively to sanction such police incursion into privacy it would run counter to the guaranty of the Fourteenth Amendment." At p. 28.

Nevertheless, after declaring that the "security of one's privacy against arbitrary intrusion by the police" is "implicit in 'the concept of ordered liberty' and as such enforceable against the States through the Due Process Clause," cf. *Palko v. Connecticut*, 302 U.S. 319 (1937), and announcing that it "stoutly adhere[d]" to the *Weeks* decision, the Court decided that the *Weeks* exclusionary rule would not then be imposed upon the States as "an essential ingredient of the right." 338 U.S., at 27–29. The Court's reasons for not considering essential to the right to privacy, as a curb imposed upon the States by the Due Process Clause, that which decades before had been posited as part and parcel of the Fourth Amendment's limitation upon federal encroachment of individual privacy, were bottomed on factual considerations. . . .

The Court in *Wolf* first stated that "[t]he contrariety of views of the States" on the adoption of the exclusionary rule of *Weeks* was "particularly impressive" (at p. 29); and, in this connection, that it could not "brush aside the experience of States which deem the incidence of such conduct by the police too slight to call for a deterrent remedy . . . by overriding the [States'] relevant rules of evidence." At pp. 31–32. While in 1949, prior to the *Wolf* case, almost two-thirds of the States were opposed to the use of the exclusionary rule, now, despite the *Wolf* case, more than half of those since passing upon it, by their own legislative or judicial decision, have wholly or partly adopted or adhered to the *Weeks* rule. See *Elkins v. United States*, 364 U.S. 206, Appendix, pp. 224–232 (1960). Significantly, among those now following the rule is California, which, according to its highest court, was "compelled to reach that conclusion because other remedies have completely failed to secure compliance with the constitutional provisions. . . ." *People v. Cahan*, 44 Cal. 2d 434, 445, 282 P. 2d 905, 911 (1955). In connection with this California case, we note that the second basis elaborated in *Wolf* in support of its failure to enforce the exclusionary doctrine against the States was that "other means of protection" have been afforded "the right to privacy." 338 U.S., at 30. The experience of California that such other remedies have been worthless and futile is buttressed by the experience of other States. The obvious futility of relegating the Fourth Amendment to the protection of other remedies has, moreover, been recognized by this Court since *Wolf*. See *Irvine v. California*, 347 U.S. 128, 137 (1954). . . .

It, therefore, plainly appears that the factual considerations supporting the failure of the *Wolf* Court to include the *Weeks* exclusionary rule when it recognized the enforceability of the right to privacy against the States in 1949, while not basically relevant to the constitutional consideration, could not, in any analysis, now be deemed controlling. . . .

Since the Fourth Amendment's right of privacy has been declared enforceable against the States through the Due Process Clause of the Fourteenth, it is enforceable against them by the same sanction of exclusion as is used against the Federal Government. Were it otherwise, then just as without the *Weeks* rule the assurance against unreasonable federal searches and seizures would be "a form of words," valueless and undeserving of mention in a perpetual charter of inestimable human liberties, so too, without that rule the freedom from state invasions of privacy would be so ephemeral and so neatly severed from its conceptual nexus with the freedom from all brutish means of coercing evidence as not to merit this Court's high regard as a freedom "implicit in the concept of ordered liberty." At the time that the Court held in *Wolf* that the Amendment was applicable to the States through the Due Process Clause, the cases of this Court, as we have seen, had steadfastly held that as to federal officers the Fourth Amendment included the exclusion of the evidence seized in violation of its provisions. Even *Wolf* "stoutly adhered" to that proposition. The right to privacy, when conceded operatively enforceable against the States, was not susceptible of destruction by avulsion of the sanction upon which its protection and enjoyment had always been deemed dependent under the *Boyd*, *Weeks* and *Silverthorne* cases. Therefore, in extending the substantive protections of due process to all constitutionally unreasonable searches—state or federal—it was logically and constitutionally necessary that the exclusion doctrine—an essential part of the right to privacy—be also insisted upon as an essential ingredient of the right newly recognized by the *Wolf* case. In short, the admission of the new constitutional right by *Wolf* could not consistently tolerate denial of its most important constitutional privilege, namely, the exclusion of the evidence which an accused had been forced to give by reason of the unlawful seizure. To hold otherwise is to grant the right but in reality to withhold its privilege and enjoyment. Only last year the Court itself recognized that the purpose of the exclusionary rule "is to deter—to compel respect for the constitutional guaranty in the only effectively available way—by removing the incentive to disregard it." *Elkins v. United States, supra*, at 217. . . .

The judgment of the Supreme Court of Ohio is reversed and the cause remanded for further proceedings not inconsistent with this opinion.

Reversed and remanded.

UNITED STATES v. LEON
468 U.S. 897 (1984)

JUSTICE WHITE delivered the opinion of the Court.

This case presents the question whether the Fourth Amendment exclusionary rule should be modified so as not to bar the use in the prosecution's case in chief of evidence obtained by officers acting in reasonable reliance on a search warrant issued by a detached and neutral magistrate but ultimately found to be unsupported by probable cause. To resolve this question, we must consider once again the tension between the sometimes competing goals of, on the one hand, deterring official misconduct and removing inducements to unreasonable invasions of privacy and, on the other, establishing procedures under which criminal defendants are "acquitted or convicted on the basis of all the evidence which exposes the truth." *Alderman v. United States*, 394 U.S. 165, 175 (1969).

In August 1981, a confidential informant of unproven reliability informed an officer of the Burbank Police Department that two persons known to him as "Armando" and "Patsy" were selling large quantities of cocaine and methaqualone from their residence at 620 Price Drive in Burbank, Cal. The informant also indicated that he had witnessed a sale of methaqualone by "Patsy" at the residence approximately five months earlier and had observed at that time a shoebox containing a large amount of cash that belonged to "Patsy." He further declared that "Armando" and "Patsy" generally kept only small quantities of drugs at their residence and stored the remainder at another location in Burbank.

On the basis of this information, the Burbank police initiated an extensive investigation focusing first on the Price Drive residence and later on two other residences as well. Cars parked at the Price Drive residence were determined to belong to respondents Armando Sanchez, who had previously been arrested for possession of marihuana, and Patsy Stewart, who had no criminal record. During the course of the investigation, officers observed an automobile belonging to respondent Ricardo Del Castillo, who had previously been arrested for possession of 50 pounds of marihuana, arrive at the Price Drive residence. The driver of that car entered the house, exited shortly thereafter carrying a small paper sack, and drove away. A check of Del Castillo's probation records led the officers to respondent Alberto Leon, whose telephone number Del Castillo had listed as his employer's. Leon had been arrested in 1980 on drug charges, and a companion had informed the police at that time that Leon was heavily involved in the importation of drugs into this country. Before the current investigation began, the Burbank officers had learned that an informant had told a Glendale police officer that Leon stored a large quantity of methaqualone at his residence in Glendale. During the course of this investigation, the Burbank officers learned that Leon was living at 716 South Sunset Canyon in Burbank.

Subsequently, the officers observed several persons, at least one of whom had prior drug involvement, arriving at the Price Drive residence and leaving with small packages; observed a variety of other material activity at the two residences as well as at a condominium at 7902 Via Magdalena; and witnessed a variety of relevant activity involving respondents' automobiles. The officers also observed respondents Sanchez and Stewart board separate flights for Miami. The pair later returned to Los Angeles together, consented to a search of their luggage that revealed only a small amount of marihuana, and left the airport. Based on these and other observations summarized in the affidavit, . . . Officer Cyril Rombach of the Burbank Police Department, an experienced and well-trained narcotics investigator, prepared an application for a warrant to search 620 Price Drive, 716 South Sunset Canyon, 7902 Via Magdalena, and automobiles registered to each of the respondents for an extensive list of items believed to be related to respondents' drug-trafficking activities. Officer Rombach's extensive application was reviewed by several Deputy District Attorneys.

A facially valid search warrant was issued in September 1981 by a State Superior Court Judge. The ensuing searches produced large quantities of drugs at the Via Magdalena and Sunset Canyon addresses and a small quantity at the Price Drive residence. Other evidence was discovered at each of the residences and in Stewart's and Del Castillo's automobiles. Respondents were indicted by a grand jury in the District Court for the Central District of California and charged with conspiracy to possess and distribute cocaine and a variety of substantive counts.

The respondents then filed motions to suppress the evidence seized pursuant to the warrant. The District Court held an evidentiary hearing and, while recognizing that the case was a close one, . . . granted the motions to suppress in part. It concluded that the affidavit was insufficient to establish probable cause, but did not suppress all of the evidence as to all of the respondents because none of the respondents had standing to challenge all of the searches. In response to a request from the Government, the court made clear that Officer Rombach had acted in good faith, but it rejected the Government's suggestion that the Fourth Amendment exclusionary rule should not apply where evidence is seized in reasonable, good-faith reliance on a search warrant. . . .

Whether the exclusionary sanction is appropriately imposed in a particular case, our decisions make clear, is "an issue separate from the question whether the Fourth Amendment rights of the party seeking to invoke the rule were violated by police conduct." *Illinois v. Gates, supra,* at 223. Only the former question is currently before us, and it must be resolved by weighing the costs and benefits of preventing the use in the prosecution's case in chief of inherently trustworthy tangible evidence obtained in reliance on a search warrant issued by a detached and neutral magistrate that ultimately is found to be defective.

The substantial social costs exacted by the exclusionary rule for the vindication of Fourth Amendment rights have long been a source of concern. "Our cases have consistently recognized that unbending application of the exclusionary sanction to enforce ideals of governmental rectitude would impede unacceptably the truth-finding functions of judge and jury." *United States v. Payner,* 447 U.S. 727, 734 (1980). An objectionable collateral consequence of this interference with the criminal justice system's truth-finding function is that some guilty defendants may go free or receive reduced sentences as a result of favorable plea bargains. Particularly when law enforcement officers have acted in objective good faith or their transgressions have been minor, the magnitude of the benefit conferred on such guilty defendants offends basic concepts of the criminal justice system. *Stone v. Powell*, 428 U.S., at 490. Indiscriminate application of the exclusionary rule, therefore, may well "generat[e] disrespect for the law and administration of justice." *Id.*, at 491. Accordingly, "[a]s with any remedial device, the application of the rule has been restricted to those areas where its remedial objectives are thought most efficaciously served." *United States v. Calandra, supra*, at 348; see *Stone v. Powell, supra*, at 486–487; *United States v. Janis*, 428 U.S. 433, 447 (1976). . . .

Because a search warrant "provides the detached scrutiny of a neutral magistrate, which is a more reliable safeguard against improper searches than the hurried judgment of a law enforcement officer 'engaged in the often competitive enterprise of ferreting out crime,'" *United States v. Chadwick*, 433 U.S. 1, 9 (1977) (quoting *Johnson v. United States*, 333 U.S. 10, 14 (1948)), we have expressed a strong preference for warrants and declared that "in a doubtful or marginal case a search under a warrant may be sustainable where without one it would fall." . . .

Deference to the magistrate, however, is not boundless. It is clear, first, that the deference accorded to a magistrate's finding of probable cause does not preclude inquiry into the knowing or reckless falsity of the affidavit on which that determination was based. *Franks v. Delaware*, 438 U.S. 154 (1978). Second, the courts must also insist that the magistrate purport to "perform his 'neutral and detached' function and not serve merely as a rubber stamp for the police." . . .

Third, reviewing courts will not defer to a warrant based on an affidavit that does not "provide the magistrate with a substantial basis for determining the existence of probable cause." *Illinois v. Gates*, 462 U.S., at 239. "Sufficient information must be presented to the magistrate to allow that official to determine probable cause; his action cannot be a mere ratification of the bare conclusions of others." *Ibid.* See *Aguilar v. Texas, supra*, at 114–115; *Giordenello v. United States*, 357 U.S. 480 (1958); *Nathanson v. United States*, 290 U.S. 41 (1933). Even if the warrant application was supported by more than a "bare bones" affidavit, a reviewing court may properly conclude that, notwithstanding the deference that magistrates deserve, the warrant was invalid because the magistrate's probable-cause determination reflected an improper analysis of the totality of the circumstances, *Illinois v. Gates, supra*, at 238–239, or because the form of the warrant was improper in some respect.

Only in the first of these three situations, however, has the Court set forth a rationale for suppressing evidence obtained pursuant to a search warrant; in the other areas, it has simply excluded such evidence without considering whether Fourth Amendment interests will be advanced. To the extent that proponents of exclusion rely on its behavioral effects on judges and magistrates in these areas, their reliance is misplaced. First, the exclusionary rule is designed to deter police misconduct rather than to punish the errors of judges and magistrates. Second, there exists no evidence suggesting that judges and magistrates are inclined to ignore or subvert the Fourth Amendment or that lawlessness among these actors requires application of the extreme sanction of exclusion.

Third, and most important, we discern no basis, and are offered none, for believing that exclusion of evidence seized pursuant to a warrant will have a significant deterrent effect on the issuing judge or magistrate. Many of the factors that indicate that the exclusionary rule cannot provide an effective "special" or "general" deterrent for individual offending law enforcement officers apply as well to judges or magistrates. And, to the extent that the rule is thought to operate as a "systemic" deterrent on a wider audience, it clearly can have no such effect on individuals empowered to issue search warrants. . . . The threat of exclusion thus cannot be expected significantly to deter them. Imposition of the exclusionary sanction is not necessary meaningfully to inform judicial officers of their errors, and we cannot conclude that admitting evidence obtained pursuant to a warrant while at the same time declaring that the warrant was somehow defective will in any way reduce judicial officers' professional incentives to comply with the Fourth Amendment, encourage them to repeat their mistakes, or lead to the granting of all colorable warrant requests. . . .

We conclude that the marginal or nonexistent benefits produced by suppressing evidence obtained in objectively reasonable reliance on a subsequently invalidated search warrant cannot justify the substantial costs of exclusion. . . .

Suppression therefore remains an appropriate remedy if the magistrate or judge in issuing a warrant was misled by information in an affidavit that the affiant knew was false or would have known was false except for his reckless disregard of the truth. *Franks v. Delaware*, 438 U.S. 154 (1978). The exception we recognize today will also not apply in cases where the issuing magistrate wholly abandoned his judicial role in the manner condemned in *Lo-Ji Sales, Inc. v. New York*, 442 U.S. 319 (1979); in such circumstances, no reasonably well trained officer should rely on the warrant. Nor would an officer manifest objective good faith in relying on a warrant based on an affidavit "so lacking in indicia of probable cause as to render official belief in its existence entirely unreasonable." *Brown v. Illinois*, 422 U.S., at 610–611 (Powell, J. concurring in part); see *Illinois v. Gates, supra*, at 263–264 (White, J., concurring in judgment). Finally, depending on the circumstances of the particular case, a warrant may be so facially deficient—*i.e.*, in failing to particularize the place to be searched or the things to be seized—that the executing officers cannot reasonably presume it to be valid. Cf. *Massachusetts v. Sheppard, post*, at 988–991.

In so limiting the suppression remedy, we leave untouched the probable-cause standard and the various requirements for a valid warrant. Other objections to the modification of the Fourth Amendment exclusionary rule we consider to be insubstantial. The good-faith exception for searches conducted pursuant to warrants is not intended to signal our unwillingness strictly to enforce the requirements of the Fourth Amendment, and we do not believe that it will have this effect. As we have already suggested, the good-faith exception, turning as it does on objective reasonableness, should not be difficult to apply in practice. When officers have acted pursuant to a warrant, the prosecution should ordinarily be able to establish objective good faith without a substantial expenditure of judicial time. . . .

When the principles we have enunciated today are applied to the facts of this case, it is apparent that the judgment of the Court of Appeals cannot stand. The Court of Appeals applied the prevailing legal standards to Officer Rombach's warrant application and concluded that the application could not support the magistrate's probable-cause determination. In so doing, the court clearly informed the magistrate that he had erred in issuing the challenged warrant. This aspect of the court's judgment is not under attack in this proceeding. . . .

In the absence of an allegation that the magistrate abandoned his detached and neutral role, suppression is appropriate only if the officers were dishonest or reckless in preparing their affidavit or could not have harbored an objectively reasonable belief in the existence of probable cause. Only respondent Leon has contended that no reasonably well trained police officer could have believed that there existed probable cause to search his house; significantly, the other respondents advance no comparable argument. Officer Rombach's application for a warrant clearly was supported by much more than a "bare bones" affidavit. The affidavit related the results of an extensive investigation and, as the opinions of the divided panel of the Court of Appeals make clear, provided evidence sufficient to create disagreement among thoughtful and competent judges as to the existence of probable cause. Under these circumstances, the officers' reliance on the magistrate's determination of probable cause was objectively reasonable, and application of the extreme sanction of exclusion is inappropriate.

Accordingly, the judgment of the Court of Appeals is

Reversed.

..............................DISCUSSION QUESTIONS..............................

1. The exclusionary rule has been the only way the Supreme Court has been able to enforce the Fourth Amendment. What are the other options and why don't they seem to work?

2. The Court was reluctant to impose the exclusionary rule on the states. Why do you think the facts of the case of *Mapp v. Ohio* changed their minds on this issue?

3. People whose Fourth Amendment rights have been violated may sue those who caused the violation. Generally, only the innocent may really take advantage of this option. Why?

4. In *United States v. Leon* the Court ruled that trial judges may not exclude evidence obtained with a search warrant simply because the trial judge disagrees that probable cause existed at the time the warrant was signed. Why did the Supreme Court come to this conclusion?

5. In the case of *Illinois v. Rodriguez*, the majority of justices ruled that to exclude evidence when the police make an honest mistake would accomplish nothing. The dissenting justices thought that people have a right to be secure in their homes from warrantless searches, regardless of why the police mistakenly believe they have the authority to enter. What do you think? How will people go about proving that the police made a "dishonest" rather than an "honest" mistake?

CHAPTER
seven
❋ ❋ ❋ ❋ ❋ ❋ ❋ ❋

Privacy Beyond Search
and Seizure

.... DISCUSSION ....

During the 1950s and 1960s, in interpreting the Fourth Amendment the Supreme Court began to emphasize the need to protect privacy. While earlier Courts had ruled that the Fourth Amendment protects both property and privacy, the Warren Court began to see the protection of privacy as the amendment's primary objective. The main purpose of the Fourth Amendment, as the Warren Court saw it, was to draw a line between the sphere of life that is private and the sphere of life into which government may interject itself. This meant that in interpreting the Fourth Amendment, the Court would have to decide where police could go without a warrant, and, beginning in 1965, which personal decisions government could interfere with.

CREATING THE GENERAL RIGHT TO PRIVACY

In 1965 the Court began to expand the concept of a constitutional right to privacy beyond the borders of search and seizure. The case of *Griswold v. Connecticut* (see p. 126) concerned a Connecticut statute that made it a crime to sell or prescribe contraceptives to women. Estelle Griswold, the director of a Planned Parenthood clinic, and Dr. Buxton, the prescribing physician, were convicted of prescribing a contraceptive to a married woman at the clinic. Their convictions were overturned by the U.S. Supreme Court.

Justice Douglas wrote an opinion, joined by Justice Clark, in which he ruled that there was a general right of privacy contained in the U.S. Constitution. While the actual word "privacy" does not appear in the Bill of Rights, it was clear to Justice Douglas that many of the amendments in the Bill of Rights were concerned with protecting this general right. For example, the First Amendment protects the right of free speech and religion, which could be seen as the right to think and believe private thoughts. The Third Amendment, which outlaws the quartering of soldiers in private homes, relates to the concern for privacy, as do the Fourth Amendment, which outlaws unreasonable searches and seizures, and the Fifth Amendment, which protects against being forced to incriminate yourself. He went on to say that "specific guarantees in the Bill of Rights have penumbras, formed by emanations from those guarantees that help give them life and substance." In Justice Douglas's opinion, a general right of privacy emanated from the Bill of Rights.

Justice Goldberg wrote a concurring opinion, joined by Chief Justice Warren and Justice Brennan, in which he agreed that there is a right of privacy protected by the Constitution, but he did not find this right of privacy in the same places Justice Douglas did. Instead, Justice Goldberg focused on the Ninth Amendment, which states that "The enumeration in the Constitution, of certain rights, shall not be construed to deny or disparage others retained by the people." In writing amendments to the Constitution, James Madison was concerned that later generations would think that the only rights they had were those specifically listed in the Bill of Rights. The Ninth Amendment was designed to prevent that from happening. Justice Goldberg, along with Justice Brennan and Chief Justice Warren, was prepared to find a general right to privacy protected by the Ninth Amendment.

Justices Harlan and White agreed that the Connecticut statute at issue in the *Griswold* case should be declared unconstitutional, but they refused to find a "right to privacy" in the Constitution. Instead, they thought the Fourteenth Amendment's general protection of liberty was enough to overturn this particular statute. They appeared to be relying on the same conception of the Fourteenth Amendment that the Court had used between the Civil War and the Great Depression to strike down any statutes they found disagreeable.

Justices Black and Stewart dissented. They did not think there was a right to privacy in the Constitution, and they certainly did not wish to return to the days when a majority of justices could simply use the Fourteenth Amendment to overturn any statute with which they disagreed. The Fourteenth Amendment had been used to overturn much badly needed social legislation before World War II. Justice Black said, "I like my privacy as well as the next one, but I am nevertheless compelled to admit that government has a right to invade it unless prohibited by some specific constitutional provision." Justice Stewart found the Connecticut law to be "uncommonly silly," but he could not find it to be unconstitutional.

The five-justice majority was not willing to allow Connecticut to pros-ecute doctors for counseling married women about contraception, and it was not willing to overturn the statute for violating some vague concept of "liberty" that the Fourteenth Amendment protects. These justices argued that the Fourteenth Amendment protects a more limited set of "liberties," and that, in general, these liberties would be found in the Bill of Rights. In an effort to limit the reach of their decision, they tried to confine it to what they considered the most private of realms, the marital bedroom.

Justice Douglas suggested that what the Court was really doing was antici-pating the need to invoke the Fourth Amendment. He asked: "Would we allow the police to search the sacred precincts of marital bedrooms for telltale signs of the use of contraceptives? The very idea is repulsive to the notions of privacy surrounding the marriage relationship." At the same time, the Court was clearly doing much more than outlawing an "unreasonable search and seizure." There had been no search of the "sacred precincts of marital bed-rooms" in this case.

THE RIGHT TO HAVE AN ABORTION

What would turn out to be the most difficult and socially divisive area for the Court was the question of the right to have an abortion. The original abortion decision, *Roe v. Wade*, was not easy to make. The case was originally argued in December 1971, reargued in October 1972, and decided in January 1973. An anonymous "pregnant, single woman" who could not obtain an abortion in Texas because Texas statutes only allowed abortions if they were necessary to save the life of the mother brought the case. Seven justices agreed that the right to privacy included the right to obtain an abortion.

Justice Blackmun, writing for the majority, pointed out that throughout the history of English law a person was not considered to have any rights until birth, and he ruled that this concept would continue to be in force in the United States. Because Justice Blackmun ruled that the fetus did not have any rights, *Roe* was not a case of deciding between the rights of the mother and the rights of the fetus. It was instead a case of balancing the rights of the mother against the interests of the state.

Justice Blackmun believed that the state of Texas had two valid interests in this case: an interest in regulating medical procedures to make sure they are safe and an interest in protecting "potential life." These legitimate state interests had to be weighed against the rights of the mother. He ruled that the general right of privacy outlined in Griswold was "broad enough to encompass a woman's decision whether or not to terminate her pregnancy."

In setting up a system to balance the rights of the mother against the interests of the state, Justice Blackmun developed the trimester system, breaking the nine-month pregnancy period into three periods of three months each. During the first trimester, the mother's right to privacy outweighs the state's interest in protecting potential life or the health of the mother. During the second trimester, the state may regulate abortions more closely to protect the health of the mother. During the third trimester, when the fetus is capable of living outside the womb, the state may step in to protect its interest in potential life. He ruled that during the period after the fetus is viable outside of the womb the state may "go so far as to proscribe abortion . . . except when it is necessary to preserve the life or health of the mother." While the Court overturned Texas's abortion law, it was too late for the particular woman involved in this case. Presumably she had obtained an abortion somewhere else by the time the Court made its decision.

Justices White and Rehnquist dissented. Justice White could not agree that the Constitution "values the convenience, whim, or caprice of the putative mother more than the life or potential life of the fetus." Justice Rehnquist refused to expand the right to privacy in such a way. While he did believe that the right to privacy would prevent states from outlawing abortions when a mother's life was in danger, he did not believe it could be expanded beyond that.

It is important to realize that the split in this case was not between Republicans and Democrats. The dissenting justices were one Republican and one Democrat. Chief Justice Burger, a conservative Republican, agreed with the majority opinion, which was written by a Republican, Justice Blackmun. Much of the criticism of this decision, however, came from the Republican Party. People generally believed that appointments to the Supreme Court by Republican presidents after Roe v. Wade were made with an eye to seeing that the decision would someday be overturned.

During the two decades after Roe v. Wade, several states tried to see how far they could go in regulating abortions without running into the right of privacy. In a series of decisions, usually decided by either a five-to-four or six-to-three vote, a majority of justices made it clear that many regulations that the state legislatures wished to impose on the right to have an abortion were unacceptable.

In 1976, in Planned Parenthood v. Danforth, the Court struck down a Missouri law to the extent that it required the consent of a husband before a married woman could obtain an abortion. In 1979, in Bellotti v. Baird, the

Court struck down a Massachusetts law that required a woman under the age of 18 to get the permission of a parent or a judge before obtaining an abortion.

By 1983 the first woman, Justice Sandra Day O'Connor, had been appointed to the Court, and the country waited to see how she would vote on the abortion question. The case, *City of Akron v. Akron Center*, involved an ordinance by the city of Akron designed to regulate abortion clinics. The regulations required abortions after the first trimester to be performed in a hospital, unmarried minors under the age of 15 to have either parental consent or a court order before having an abortion, and doctors to inform patients of complications that might result from an abortion and wait 24 hours after the woman consented to the abortion before performing it.

A majority of justices thought these regulations were too restrictive and were simply an attempt to discourage abortions. The ordinance was overturned. Justice O'Connor wrote a dissenting opinion, joined by the two justices that dissented from *Roe v. Wade*, Justices White and Rehnquist. She began by stating her objection to the whole concept of a trimester system. She said:

> [N]either sound constitutional theory nor our need to decide cases based on the application of neutral principles can accommodate an analytical framework that varies according to the "stages" of pregnancy, where those stages, and their concomitant standards of review, differ according to the level of medical technology available when a particular challenge to state regulation occurs.

She argued that the standard should be whether or not the regulations "unduly burden the right to seek an abortion." In her opinion, this concept was more direct and straightforward and should be applied throughout the pregnancy without reference to the trimester system.

Chief Justice Burger voted with the majority in both the *Roe v. Wade* and the *City of Akron* cases, but in 1986 he became the fourth dissenter in *Thornburgh v. American College of Obstetricians and Gynecologists*. In this case, a group of doctors sued to stop the enforcement of a new Pennsylvania law that required a doctor performing an abortion to receive the "informed consent" of the woman before performing an abortion. The statute required the doctor to present the woman with information about the dangers of abortions and the alternatives to abortion such as adoption, including a list of agencies that were prepared to help a woman maintain her pregnancy. The five-justice majority believed this was just another attempt by Pennsylvania to limit the right to receive an abortion.

Chief Justice Burger dissented, along with Justices White, Rehnquist, and O'Connor. When he voted for *Roe v. Wade*, Chief Justice Burger believed he was upholding the fundamental right of a woman to control her own body, but not the right to receive "abortion on demand." In the *Thornburgh* case, he did not think the majority accepted the idea that states have legitimate interests in regulating abortions, and he was particularly unhappy that the majority was not even willing to allow a state to require "that a woman contemplating an abortion be provided with accurate medical information concerning the risks inherent in the medical procedure which she is about to undergo."

By 1989 conservative justices Scalia and Kennedy had been added to the Court. The case of *Webster v. Reproductive Services* involved whether the state of Missouri could refuse to allow public employees and public hospitals to perform "nontherapeutic abortions." A majority of justices ruled that it could, and that the statute could state that after 20 weeks of pregnancy a fetus would be presumed to be viable. The vote was five to four. The majority did not find it necessary to overturn *Roe v. Wade* to reach this result, but many states assumed that this decision signaled that the Court was about to make a fundamental change in this area of the law. These states passed very restrictive abortion statutes in anticipation of this change.

REDEFINING THE RIGHT TO HAVE AN ABORTION

It was clear that the majority of justices was no longer willing to live with the expansive interpretation of the right to receive an abortion that the Court developed in the years following *Roe v. Wade*. But what would the more conservative Court do in this area? It had basically three choices.

First, the Court could reject the entire idea of a constitutional right to privacy and throw out both the right to receive contraceptives and the right to have an abortion. This would be the most drastic change and would constitute a complete break with the past.

Second, the Court could keep the basic right to privacy but rule that that right does not include the right to have an abortion, presumably because an abortion involves the life of another person, the fetus. While less drastic, this would mean rejecting a clear holding by seven justices, apparently for the sole reason that a new group of justices did not agree with that holding. While past Courts had certainly overturned prior decisions, in almost every case the new decision broadened the rights of individuals under the Constitution. This would be a rare case of actually contracting individual rights after those rights had been discovered by the Court and relied upon by the people.

Third, the Court could continue to support the right of privacy and the right to obtain an abortion but modify the way that right would be protected.

Justice O'Connor had been arguing since 1983 that the test in this area should be whether a regulation is unduly burdensome to the right to receive an abortion. If this new test were adopted, many of the regulations that had been rejected by the Court between 1973 and the end of the 1980s would be allowed, but some presumably would still be beyond the power of the states. As it turned out, in June 1992 the Court took the third approach.

In *Planned Parenthood v. Casey*, (see p. 129) the Court ruled five to four that the right to an abortion would still exist. The case had been brought by abortion clinics objecting to several provisions in Pennsylvania's new abortion control statute. Particularly, the clinics objected to the requirements that women wait 24 hours before being given an abortion, that young women be required to obtain parental consent or a court order before obtaining an abortion, and that husbands be notified before an abortion could be carried out.

Chief Justice Rehnquist and Justices White, Scalia, and Thomas were ready to reject the idea that the right to privacy protects a right to have an abortion and find the Pennsylvania law to be constitutional. Justices Blackmun and Stevens were ready to support *Roe v. Wade* as it had been interpreted and find most of these requirements to be in violation of *Roe's* provisions.

Justices O'Connor, Kennedy, and Souter, who formed the deciding block of justices, were not prepared to agree with either of these extreme positions. They delivered an unusual joint opinion, signed by all three justices. Their opinion began with the statement that "Liberty finds no refuge in a jurisprudence of doubt." They pointed out that two decades after the *Roe v. Wade* decision there was still much doubt about the extent to which the Constitution protects a woman's right to terminate a pregnancy in its early stages. *Roe v. Wade* would be modified but affirmed.

These justices affirmed several parts of the *Roe* decision. First, women have a right to have an abortion before the fetus becomes viable and to "obtain it without undue interference from the State." Second, the state may outlaw abortions after viability as long as the law allows exceptions if the woman's life or health is in danger. Third, the state does have legitimate interests at the beginning of a pregnancy in protecting both the woman and the fetus.

They also reaffirmed the idea that there is a general right to privacy, which is protected by the Constitution. They pointed out that "it is a premise of the Constitution that there is a realm of personal liberty which the government may not enter" and that this realm of personal liberty includes liberties related to marriage and reproduction. In defining what this realm of personal liberty included, these justices argued that the justices must avoid simply invalidating state laws with which they disagree, but at the same time they must not shrink from the duties of their office. They went on to say:

> Our law affords constitutional protection to personal decisions relating to marriage, procreation, contraception, family relationships, child rearing, and education. . . . Our cases recognize "the right of the individual, married or single, to be free from unwarranted governmental intrusion into matters so fundamentally affecting a person as the decision whether to bear or beget a child." . . . Our precedents "have respected the private realm of family life which the state cannot enter." . . . These matters, involving the most intimate and personal choices a person may make in a lifetime, choices central to personal dignity and autonomy, are central to the liberty protected by the Fourteenth Amendment. At the heart of liberty is the right to define one's own concept of existence, of meaning, of the universe, and of the mystery of human life. Beliefs about these matters could not define the attributes of personhood were they formed under compulsion of the State.

Justices O'Connor, Kennedy, and Souter then affirmed that the right to privacy included the right to have an abortion, which means states may not place an undue burden on the right to have an abortion.

However, these justices then ruled that some of the specific aspects of *Roe v. Wade* had been ineffective. The trimester system had proven particularly unworkable and was rejected by these justices. In the future the key would be viability, whether or not the fetus was capable of life outside the womb. Until the fetus was viable, states would not be allowed to impose an undue burden on the woman's right to obtain an abortion. After that time, the state could outlaw abortions except in cases where the life or health of the mother is threatened.

These justices accepted the idea that the state's legitimate interests could justify reasonable regulations of the abortion process before viability. In this case, they upheld Pennsylvania's 24-hour waiting period and the requirement that a minor receive either parental permission or demonstrate to a judge that she is capable of making an informed decision on her own before obtaining an abortion. In the opinion of these justices, these provisions were not an "undue burden" on the right of privacy. This part of the decision overturned previous decisions by the Court that had held similar provisions to be a violation of the right to privacy.

On the other hand, these justices did find the requirement that a married woman obtain the signed consent of her spouse before obtaining an abortion to be an undue burden on her right to privacy. The findings of the trial judge that violence and abuse might result from such a requirement were compelling. Given the possibility of both physical and psychological abuse against the woman by the husband and the many different circumstances in which pregnant women find themselves, the requirement of spousal consent would be an undue burden on the woman's right to decide for herself what she could do with her own body. The justices pointed out that under U.S. law married women are no longer considered to be just an extension of their husbands but rather independent individuals with their own constitutional rights.

CONCLUSION

Beginning with the *Griswold* decision in 1965 and ending with the *Planned Parenthood* decision in 1992, the Court struggled to expand the right to privacy beyond the realm of search and seizure, and to do this in a way that would both protect the fundamental principles of individual rights and provide guidance for future Supreme Courts. The Court appears to have accomplished that goal. The expanded right to privacy includes the right of individuals to make such fundamental decisions as whether or not to have a child. The general right to privacy distinguished between decisions that must be made by the individual and decisions that the state may legitimately control. Whether the general right to privacy will expand further in the years to come remains to be seen.

CASE DECISIONS

Griswold v. Connecticut stands for the proposition that the Bill of Rights and the Fourteenth Amendment protect a general right of privacy, which grows out of the specific rights protected in the Bill of Rights. Justice Douglas wrote the opinion for the Court and Justice Goldberg wrote a concurring opinion, both of which are included here. Justices Harlan and White wrote concurring opinions, which are not included. Justice Black's and Justice Stewart's dissenting opinions are not included.

Planned Parenthood v. Casey reaffirmed the proposition that there is a general right to privacy protected by the Bill of Rights and the Fourteenth Amendment and that this right includes the right to have an abortion. Justices O'Connor, Kennedy, and Souter wrote an unusual joint opinion for the Court, which is included here. Justices Stevens, Blackmun, and Scalia and Chief Justice Rehnquist wrote opinions that concurred with part of the joint opinion and dissented from part of it. These opinions are not included here.

Following are excerpts from the case decisions.

❊ ❊ ❊ ❊ ❊ ❊ ❊ ❊ ❊

GRISWOLD v. CONNECTICUT
381 U.S. 479 (1965)

MR. JUSTICE DOUGLAS delivered the opinion of the Court.

Appellant Griswold is Executive Director of the Planned Parenthood League of Connecticut. Appellant Buxton is a licensed physician and a professor at the Yale Medical School who served as Medical Director for the League at its Center in New Haven—a center open and operating from November 1 to November 10, 1961, when appellants were arrested.

They gave information, instruction, and medical advice to *married persons* as to the means of preventing conception. They examined the wife and prescribed the best contraceptive device or material for her use. Fees were usually charged, although some couples were serviced free.

The statutes whose constitutionality is involved in this appeal are §§ 53–32 and 54–196 of the General Statutes of Connecticut (1958 rev.). The former provides:

> "Any person who uses any drug, medicinal article or instrument for the purpose of preventing conception shall be fined not less than fifty dollars or imprisoned not less than sixty days nor more than one year or be both fined and imprisoned."

Section 54–196 provides:

> "Any person who assists, abets, counsels, causes, hires or commands another to commit any offense may be prosecuted and punished as if he were the principal offender."

The appellants were found guilty as accessories and fined $100 each, against the claim that the accessory statute as so applied violated the Fourteenth Amendment. The Appellate Division of the Circuit Court affirmed. The Supreme Court of Errors affirmed that judgment. 151 Conn. 544, 200 A. 2d 479. We noted probable jurisdiction. 379 U.S. 926. . . .

[S]pecific guarantees in the Bill of Rights have penumbras, formed by emanations from those guarantees that help give them life and substance. See *Poe v. Ullman*, 367 U.S. 497, 516–522 (dissenting opinion). Various guarantees create zones of privacy. The right of association contained in the penumbra of the First Amendment is one. . . . The Third Amendment in its prohibition against the quartering of soldiers "in any house" in time of peace without the consent of the owner is another facet of that privacy. The Fourth Amendment explicitly affirms the "right of the people to be secure in their persons, houses, papers, and effects, against unreasonable searches and seizures." The Fifth Amendment in its Self-Incrimination Clause enables the citizen to create a zone of privacy which government may not force him to surrender to his detriment. The Ninth Amendment provides: "The enumeration in the Constitution, of certain rights, shall not be construed to deny or disparage others retained by the people."

The Fourth and Fifth Amendments were described in *Boyd v. United States*, 116 U.S. 616, 630, as protection against all governmental invasions "of the sanctity of a man's home and the privacies of life." We recently referred in *Mapp v. Ohio*, 367 U.S. 643, 656, to the Fourth Amendment as creating a "right to privacy, no less important than any other right carefully and particularly reserved to the people." See Beaney, The Constitutional Right to Privacy, 1962 Sup.Ct.Rev. 212; Griswold, The Right to be Let Alone, 55 Nw.U.L.Rev. 216 (1960). . . .

The present case, then, concerns a relationship lying within the zone of privacy created by several fundamental constitutional guarantees. And it concerns a law which, in forbidding the *use* of contraceptives rather than regulating their manufacture or sale, seeks to achieve its goals by means having a maximum destructive impact upon that relationship. Such a law cannot stand in light of the familiar principle, so often applied by this Court, that a "governmental purpose to control or prevent activities constitutionally subject to state regulation may not be achieved by means which sweep unnecessarily broadly and thereby invade the area of protected freedoms." *NAACP v. Alabama*, 377 U.S. 288, 307. Would we allow the police to search the sacred precincts of marital bedrooms for telltale signs of the use of contraceptives? The very idea is repulsive to the notions of privacy surrounding the marriage relationship.

We deal with a right of privacy older than the Bill of Rights—older than our political parties, older than our school system. Marriage is a coming together for better or for worse, hopefully enduring, and intimate to the degree of being sacred. It is an association that promotes a way of life, not causes; a harmony in living, not political faiths; a bilateral loyalty, not commercial or social projects. Yet it is an association for as noble a purpose as any involved in our prior decisions.

Reversed.

Concurring Opinion   MR. JUSTICE GOLDBERG, whom THE CHIEF JUSTICE and MR. JUSTICE BRENNAN join, concurring.

I agree with the Court that Connecticut's birth-control law unconstitutionally intrudes upon the right of marital privacy, and I join in its opinion and judgment. Although I have not accepted the view that "due process" as used in the Fourteenth Amendment incorporates all of the first eight Amendments (see my concurring opinion in *Pointer v. Texas*, 380 U.S. 400, 410, and the dissenting opinion of Mr. Justice Brennan in *Cohen v. Hurley*, 366 U.S. 117, 154), I do agree that the concept of liberty protects those personal rights that are fundamental, and is not confined to the specific terms of the Bill of Rights. My conclusion that the concept of liberty is not so restricted and that it embraces the right of marital privacy though that right is not mentioned explicitly in the Constitution is supported both by numerous decisions of this Court, referred to in the Court's opinion, and by the language and history of the Ninth Amendment. In reaching the conclusion that the right of marital privacy is protected, as being within the protected penumbra of specific guarantees of the Bill of Rights, the Court refers to the Ninth Amendment, *ante*, at 484. I add these words to emphasize the relevance of that Amendment to the Court's holding. . . .

This Court, in a series of decisions, has held that the Fourteenth Amendment absorbs and applies to the States those specifics of the first eight amendments which express fundamental personal rights. The language and history of the Ninth Amendment reveal that the Framers of the Constitution believed that there are additional fundamental rights, protected from governmental infringement, which exist alongside those fundamental rights specifically mentioned in the first eight constitutional amendments.

The Ninth Amendment reads, "The enumeration in the Constitution, of certain rights, shall not be construed to deny or disparage others retained by the people." The Amendment is almost entirely the work of James Madison. It was introduced in Congress by him and passed the House and Senate with little or no debate and virtually no change in language. It was proffered to quiet expressed fears that a bill of specifically enumerated rights could not be sufficiently broad to cover all essential rights and that the specific mention of certain rights would be interpreted as a denial that others were protected. . . .

In determining which rights are fundamental, judges are not left at large to decide cases in light of their personal and private notions. Rather, they must look to the "traditions and [collective] conscience of our people" to determine whether a principle is "so rooted [there] . . . as to be ranked as fundamental." *Snyder v. Massachusetts*, 291 U.S. 97, 105. The inquiry is whether a right involved "is of such a character that it cannot be denied without violating those 'fundamental principles of liberty and justice which lie at the base of all our civil and political institutions'. . . ." *Powell v. Alabama*, 287 U.S. 45, 67. "Liberty" also "gains content from the emanations of . . . specific [constitutional] guarantees" and "from experience with the requirements of a free society." *Poe v. Ullman*, 367 U.S. 497, 517 (dissenting opinion of Mr. Justice Douglas). . . .

The entire fabric of the Constitution and the purposes that clearly under-lie its specific guarantees demonstrate that the rights to marital privacy and to marry and raise a family are of similar order and magnitude as the fundamental rights specifically protected.

Although the Constitution does not speak in so many words of the right of privacy in marriage, I cannot believe that it offers these fundamental rights no protection. The fact that no particular provision of the Constitution explicitly forbids the State from disrupting the traditional relation of the family—a relation so old and as fundamental as our entire civilization—surely does not show that the Government was meant to have the power to do so. Rather, as the Ninth Amendment expressly recognizes, there are fundamental personal rights such as this one, which are protected from abridgment by the Government though not specifically mentioned in the Constitution. . . .

In sum, I believe that the right of privacy in the marital relation is fundamental and basic—a personal right "retained by the people" within the meaning of the Ninth Amendment. Connecticut cannot constitutionally abridge this fundamental right, which is protected by the Fourteenth Amendment from infringement by the States. I agree with the Court that petitioners' convictions must therefore be reversed.

PLANNED PARENTHOOD v. CASEY
112 S. Ct. 2791 (1992)

JUSTICE O'CONNOR, JUSTICE KENNEDY, and JUSTICE SOUTER announced the judgment of the Court. . . .

Liberty finds no refuge in a jurisprudence of doubt. Yet 19 years after our holding that the Constitution protects a woman's right to terminate her pregnancy in its early stages, *Roe v. Wade*, 410 U.S. 113 (1973), that definition of liberty is still questioned. Joining the respondents as *amicus curiae*, the United States, as it has done in five other cases in the last decade, again asks us to overrule *Roe*. . . .

At issue in these cases are five provisions of the Pennsylvania Abortion Control Act of 1982 as amended in 1988 and 1989. 18 Pa. Cons.Stat. §§ 3203–3220 (1990). . . . The Act requires that a woman seeking an abortion give her informed consent prior to the abortion procedure, and specifies that she be provided with certain information at least 24 hours before the abortion is performed. § 3205. For a minor to obtain an abortion, the Act requires the informed consent of one of her parents, but provides for a judicial bypass option if the minor does not wish to or cannot obtain a parent's consent. § 3206. Another provision of the Act requires that, unless certain exceptions apply, a married woman seeking an abortion must sign a statement indicating that she has notified her husband of her intended abortion. § 3209. The Act exempts compliance with these three requirements in the event of a "medical emergency," which is defined in § 3203 of the Act. See §§ 3203, 3205(a), 3206(a), 3209(c). In addition to the above provisions regulating the performance of abortions, the Act imposes certain reporting requirements on facilities that provide abortion services. §§ 3207(b), 3214(a), 3214(f).

Before any of these provisions took effect, the petitioners, who are five abortion clinics and one physician representing himself as well as a class of physicians who provide abortion services, brought this suit seeking declaratory and injunctive relief. Each provision was challenged as unconstitutional on its face. The District Court entered a preliminary injunction against the enforcement of the regulations, and, after a 3-day bench trial, held all the provisions at issue here unconstitutional, entering a permanent injunction against Pennsylvania's enforcement of them. 744 F.Supp. 1323 (ED Pa.1990). The Court of Appeals for the Third Circuit affirmed in part and reversed in part, upholding all of the regulations except for the husband notification requirement. 947 F.2d 682 (1991). . . .

The Court of Appeals found it necessary to follow an elaborate course of reasoning even to identify the first premise to use to determine whether the statute enacted by Pennsylvania meets constitutional standards. See 947 F.2d, at 687–698. And at oral argument in this Court, the attorney for the parties challenging the statute took the position that none of the enactments can be upheld without overruling Roe v. Wade. . . . We disagree with that analysis; but we acknowledge that our decisions after Roe cast doubt upon the meaning and reach of its holding. . . . State and federal courts as well as legislatures throughout the Union must have guidance as they seek to address this subject in conformance with the Constitution. Given these premises, we find it imperative to review once more the principles that define the rights of the woman and the legitimate authority of the State respecting the termination of pregnancies by abortion procedures.

After considering the fundamental constitutional questions resolved by Roe, principles of institutional integrity, and the rule of stare decisis, we are led to conclude this: the essential holding of Roe v. Wade should be retained and once again reaffirmed.

It must be stated at the outset and with clarity that Roe's essential holding, the holding we reaffirm, has three parts. First is a recognition of the right of the woman to choose to have an abortion before viability and to obtain it without undue interference from the State. Before viability, the State's interests are not strong enough to support a prohibition of abortion or the imposition of a substantial obstacle to the woman's effective right to elect the procedure. Second is a confirmation of the State's power to restrict abortions after fetal viability, if the law contains exceptions for pregnancies which endanger a woman's life or health. And third is the principle that the State has legitimate interests from the outset of the pregnancy in protecting the health of the woman and the life of the fetus that may become a child. These principles do not contradict one another; and we adhere to each.

Constitutional protection of the woman's decision to terminate her pregnancy derives from the Due Process Clause of the Fourteenth Amendment. It declares that no State shall "deprive any person of life, liberty, or property, without due process of law." The controlling word in the case before us is "liberty." Although a literal reading of the Clause might suggest that it governs only the procedures by which a State may deprive persons of liberty, for at least 105 years . . . the Clause has been understood to contain a substantive component as well, one "barring certain government actions regardless of the fairness of the procedures used to implement them." . . .

The most familiar of the substantive liberties protected by the Fourteenth Amendment are those recognized by the Bill of Rights. We have held that the Due Process Clause of the Fourteenth Amendment incorporates most of the Bill of Rights against the States. See, e.g., Duncan v. Louisiana, 391 U.S. 145, 147–148 (1968). It is tempting, as a means of curbing the discretion of federal judges, to suppose that liberty encompasses no more than those rights already guaranteed to the individual against federal interference by the express provisions of the first eight amendments to the Constitution. See Adamson v. California, 332 U.S. 46, 68–92 (1947) (Black, J., dissenting). But of course this Court has never accepted that view.

It is also tempting, for the same reason, to suppose that the Due Process Clause protects only those practices, defined at the most specific level, that were protected against government interference by other rules of law when the Fourteenth Amendment was ratified. See Michael H. v. Gerald D., 491 U.S. 110, 127–128, n. 6 (1989) (opinion of Scalia, J.). But such a view would be inconsistent with our law. It is a promise of the Constitution that there is a realm of personal liberty which the government may not enter. We have vindicated this principle before. Marriage is mentioned nowhere in the Bill of Rights and interracial marriage was illegal in most States in the 19th century, but the Court was no doubt correct in finding it to be an aspect of liberty protected against state interference by the substantive component of the Due Process Clause in Loving v. Virginia, 388 U.S. 1, 12 (1967) (relying, in an opinion for eight Justices, on the Due Process Clause). . . .

Our law affords constitutional protection to personal decisions relating to marriage, procreation, contraception, family relationships, child rearing, and education. . . . Our cases recognize "the right of the *individual*, married or single, to be free from unwarranted governmental intrusion into matters so fundamentally affecting a person as the decision whether to bear or beget a child." . . . Our precedents "have respected the private realm of family life which the state cannot enter." . . . These matters, involving the most intimate and personal choices a person may make in a lifetime, choices central to personal dignity and autonomy, are central to the liberty protected by the Fourteenth Amendment. At the heart of liberty is the right to define one's own concept of existence, of meaning, of the universe, and of the mystery of human life. Beliefs about these matters could not define the attributes of personhood were they formed under compulsion of the State.

These considerations begin our analysis of the woman's interest in terminating her pregnancy but cannot end it, for this reason: though the abortion decision may originate within the zone of conscience and belief, it is more than a philosophic exercise. Abortion is a unique act. It is an act fraught with consequences for others: for the woman who must live with the implications of her decision; for the persons who perform and assist in the procedure; for the spouse, family, and society which must confront the knowledge that these procedures exist, procedures some deem nothing short of an act of violence against innocent human life; and, depending on one's beliefs, for the life or potential life that is aborted. Though abortion is conduct, it does not follow that the State is entitled to proscribe it in all instances. That is because the liberty of the woman is at stake in a sense unique to the human condition and so unique to the law. The mother who carries a child to full term is subject to anxieties, to physical constraints, to pain that only she must bear. That these sacrifices have from the beginning of the human race been endured by woman with a pride that ennobles her in the eyes of others and gives to the infant a bond of love cannot alone be grounds for the State to insist she make the sacrifice. Her suffering is too intimate and personal for the State to insist, without more, upon its own vision of the woman's role, however dominant that vision has been in the course of our history and our culture. The destiny of the woman must be shaped to a large extent on her own conception of her spiritual imperatives and her place in society.

It should be recognized, moreover, that in some critical respects the abortion decision is of the same character as the decision to use contraception, to which *Griswold v. Connecticut*, *Eisenstadt v. Baird*, and *Carey v. Population Services International*, afford constitutional protection. We have no doubt as to the correctness of those decisions. They support the reasoning in *Roe* relating to the woman's liberty because they involve personal decisions concerning not only the meaning of procreation but also human responsibility and respect for it. As with abortion, reasonable people will have differences of opinion about these matters. One view is based on such reverence for the wonder of creation that any pregnancy ought to be welcomed and carried to full term no matter how difficult it will be to provide for the child and ensure its well-being. Another is that the inability to provide for the nurture and care of the infant is a cruelty to the child and an anguish to the parent. These are intimate views with infinite variations, and their deep, personal character underlay our decisions in *Griswold*, *Eisenstadt*, and *Carey*. The same concerns are present when the woman confronts the reality that, perhaps despite her attempts to avoid it, she has become pregnant.

It was this dimension of personal liberty that *Roe* sought to protect, and its holding invoked the reasoning and the tradition of the precedents we have discussed, granting protection to substantive liberties of the person. *Roe* was, of course, an extension of those cases and, as the decision itself indicated, the separate States could act in some degree to further their own legitimate interests in protecting pre-natal life. The extent to which the legislatures of the States might act to outweigh the interests of the woman in choosing to terminate her pregnancy was a subject of debate both in *Roe* itself and in decisions following it.

While we appreciate the weight of the arguments made on behalf of the State in the case before us, arguments which in their ultimate formulation conclude that *Roe* should be overruled, the reservations any of us may have in reaffirming the central holding of *Roe* are outweighed by the explication of individual liberty we have given combined with the force of *stare decisis*. . . .

From what we have said so far it follows that it is a constitutional liberty of the woman to have some freedom to terminate her pregnancy. We conclude that the basic decision in *Roe* was based on a constitutional analysis which we cannot now repudiate. The woman's liberty is not so unlimited, however, that from the outset the State cannot show its concern for the life of the unborn, and at a later point in fetal development the State's interest in life has sufficient force so that the right of the woman to terminate the pregnancy can be restricted.

That brings us, of course, to the point where much criticism has been directed at *Roe*, a criticism that always inheres when the Court draws a specific rule from what in the Constitution is but a general standard. We conclude, however, that the urgent claims of the woman to retain the ultimate control over her destiny and her body, claims implicit in the meaning of liberty, require us to perform that function. Liberty must not be extinguished for want of a line that is clear. And it falls to us to give some real substance to the woman's liberty to determine whether to carry her pregnancy to full term.

We conclude the line should be drawn at viability, so that before that time the woman has a right to choose to terminate her pregnancy. We adhere to this principle for two reasons. First, as we have said, is the doctrine of *stare decisis*. Any judicial act of line-drawing may seem somewhat arbitrary, but *Roe* was a reasoned statement, elaborated with great care. We have twice reaffirmed it in the face of great opposition. See *Thornburgh v. American College of Obstetricians & Gynecologists*, 476 U.S., at 759; *Akron I*, 462 U.S., at 419–120. Although we must overrule those parts of *Thornburgh* and *Akron I* which, in our view, are inconsistent with *Roe*'s statement that the State has a legitimate interest in promoting the life or potential life of the unborn, see *infra*, at _____, the central premise of those cases represents an unbroken commitment by this Court to the essential holding of *Roe*. It is that premise which we reaffirm today.

The second reason is that the concept of viability, as we noted in *Roe*, is the time at which there is a realistic possibility of maintaining and nourishing a life outside the womb, so that the independent existence of the second life can in reason and all fairness be the object of state protection that now overrides the rights of the woman. See *Roe v. Wade*, 410 U.S., at 163. Consistent with other constitutional norms, legislatures may draw lines which appear arbitrary without the necessity of offering a justification. But courts may not. We must justify the lines we draw. And there is no line other than viability which is more workable. . . .

The woman's right to terminate her pregnancy before viability is the most central principle of *Roe v. Wade*. It is a rule of law and a component of liberty we cannot renounce.

On the other side of the equation is the interest of the State in the protection of potential life. The *Roe* Court recognized the State's "important and legitimate interest in protecting the potentiality of human life." *Roe, supra*, at 162. The weight to be given this state interest, not the strength of the woman's interest, was the difficult question faced in *Roe*. We do not need to say whether each of us, had we been Members of the Court when the valuation of the State interest came before it as an original matter, would have concluded, as the *Roe* Court did, that its weight is insufficient to justify a ban on abortions prior to viability even when it is subject to certain exceptions. The matter is not before us in the first instance, and coming as it does after nearly 20 years of litigation in *Roe*'s wake we are satisfied that the immediate question is not the soundness of *Roe*'s resolution of the issue, but the precedential force that must be accorded to its holding. And we have concluded that the essential holding of *Roe* should be reaffirmed.

Yet it must be remembered that *Roe v. Wade* speaks with clarity in establishing not only the women's liberty but also the State's "important and legitimate interest in potential life." *Roe, supra*, at 163. That portion of the decision in *Roe* has been given too little acknowledgment and implementation by the Court in its subsequent cases. Those cases decided that any regulation touching upon the abortion decision must survive strict scrutiny, to be sustained only if drawn in narrow terms to further a compelling state interest. See, *e.g., Akron I, supra*, 462 U.S., at 427. Not all of the cases decided under that formulation can be reconciled with the holding in *Roe* itself that the State has legitimate interests in the health of the woman and in protecting the potential life within her. In resolving this tension, we choose to rely upon *Roe*, as against the later cases. . . .

Though the woman has a right to choose to terminate or continue her pregnancy before viability, it does not at all follow that the State is prohibited from taking steps to ensure that this choice is thoughtful and informed. Even in the earliest stages of pregnancy, the State may enact rules and regulations designed to encourage her to know that there are philosophic and social arguments of great weight that can be brought to bear in favor of continuing the pregnancy to full term and that there are procedures and institutions to allow adoption of unwanted children as well as a certain degree of state assistance if the mother chooses to raise the child herself. " '[T]he Constitution does not forbid a State or city, pursuant to democratic processes, from expressing a preference for normal childbirth.' " *Webster v. Reproductive Health Services*, 492 U.S., at 511 (opinion of the Court) (quoting *Poelker v. Doe*, 432 U.S. 519, 521 (1977)). It follows that States are free to enact laws to provide a reasonable framework for a woman to make a decision that has such profound and lasting meaning. This, too, we find consistent with *Roe*'s central premises, and indeed the inevitable consequences of our holding that the State has an interest in protecting the life of the unborn.

We reject the trimester framework, which we do not consider to be part of the essential holding of *Roe*. See *Webster v. Reproductive Health Services, supra*, 492 U.S., at 518 (opinion of Rehnquist, C.J.); *id.*, at 529 (O'Connor, J., concurring in part and concurring in judgment) (describing the trimester framework as "problematic"). Measures aimed at ensuring that a woman's choice contemplates the consequences for the fetus do not necessarily interfere with the right recognized in *Roe*, although those measures have been found to be inconsistent with the rigid trimester framework announced in that case. A logical reading of the central holding in *Roe* itself, and a necessary reconciliation of the liberty of the woman and the interest of the State in promoting prenatal life, require, in our view, that we abandon the trimester framework as a rigid prohibition on all previability regulation aimed at the protection of fetal life. The trimester framework suffers from these basic flaws: in its formulation it misconceives the nature of the pregnant woman's interest; and in practice it undervalues the State's interest in potential life, as recognized in *Roe*. . . .

The very notion that the State has a substantial interest in potential life leads to the conclusion that not all regulations must be deemed unwarranted. Not all burdens on the right to decide whether to terminate a pregnancy will be undue. In our view, the undue burden standard is the appropriate means of reconciling the State's interest with the woman's constitutionally protected liberty. . . .

What is at stake is the woman's right to make the ultimate decision, not a right to be insulated from all others in doing so. Regulations which do no more than create a structural mechanism by which the State, or the parent or guardian of a minor, may express profound respect for the life of the unborn are permitted, if they are not a substantial obstacle to the woman's exercise of the right to choose. . . . Unless it has that effect on her right of choice, a state measure designed to persuade her to choose childbirth over abortion will be upheld if reasonably related to that goal. Regulations designed to foster the health of a woman seeking an abortion are valid if they do not constitute an undue burden. . . .

We give this summary:

(a) To protect the central right recognized by *Roe v. Wade* while at the same time accommodating the State's profound interest in potential life, we will employ the undue burden analysis as explained in this opinion. An undue burden exists, and therefore a provision of law is invalid, if its purpose or effect is to place a substantial obstacle in the path of a woman seeking an abortion before the fetus attains viability.

(b) We reject the rigid trimester framework of *Roe v. Wade*. To promote the State's profound interest in potential life, throughout pregnancy the State may take measures to ensure that the woman's choice is informed, and measures designed to advance this interest will not be invalidated as long as their purpose is to persuade the woman to choose childbirth over abortion. These measures must not be an undue burden on the right.

(c) As with any medical procedure, the State may enact regulations to further the health or safety of a woman seeking an abortion. Unnecessary health regulations that have the purpose or effect of presenting a substantial obstacle to a woman seeking an abortion impose an undue burden on the right.

(d) Our adoption of the undue burden analysis does not disturb the central holding of *Roe v. Wade*, and we reaffirm that holding. Regardless of whether exceptions are made for particular circumstances, a State may not prohibit any woman from making the ultimate decision to terminate her pregnancy before viability.

(e) We also reaffirm Roe's holding that "subsequent to viability, the State in promoting its interest in the potentiality of human life may, if it chooses, regulate, and even proscribe, abortion except where it is necessary, in appropriate medical judgment, for the preservation of the life or health of the mother." . . .

These principles control our assessment of the Pennsylvania statute, and we now turn to the issue of the validity of its challenged provisions.

The Court of Appeals applied what it believed to be the undue burden standard and upheld each of the provisions except for the husband notification requirement. We agree generally with this conclusion. . . .

It is an inescapable biological fact that state regulation with respect to the child a woman is carrying will have a far greater impact on the mother's liberty than on the father's. The effect of state regulation on a woman's protected liberty is doubly deserving of scrutiny in such a case, as the State has touched not only upon the private sphere of the family but upon the very bodily integrity of the pregnant woman. . . . This conclusion rests upon the basic nature of marriage and the nature of our Constitution: "[T]he marital couple is not an independent entity with a mind and heart of its own, but an association of two individuals each with a separate intellectual and emotional makeup. If the right of privacy means anything, it is the right of the *individual*, married or single, to be free from unwarranted governmental intrusion into matters so fundamentally affecting a person as the decision whether to bear or beget a child." *Eisenstadt v. Baird*, 405 U.S., at 453 (emphasis in original). The Constitution protects individuals, men and women alike, from unjustified state interference, even when that interference is enacted into law for the benefit of their spouses.

There was a time, not so long ago, when a different understanding of the family and of the Constitution prevailed. . . . Only one generation has passed since this Court observed that "woman is still regarded as the center of home and family life," with attendant "special responsibilities" that precluded full and independent legal status under the Constitution. *Hoyt v. Florida*, 368 U.S. 57, 62 (1961). These views, of course, are no longer consistent with our understanding of the family, the individual, or the Constitution.

In keeping with our rejection of the common-law understanding of a woman's role within the family, the Court held in *Danforth* that the Constitution does not permit a State to require a married woman to obtain her husband's consent before undergoing an abortion. 428 U.S., at 69. The principles that guided the Court in *Danforth* should be our guides today. For the great many women who are victims of abuse inflicted by their husbands, or whose children are the victims of such abuse, a spousal notice requirement enables the husband to wield an effective veto over his wife's decision. Whether the prospect of notification itself deters such women from seeking abortions, or whether the husband, through physical force or psychological pressure or economic coercion, prevents his wife from obtaining an abortion until it is too late, the notice requirement will often be tantamount to the veto found unconstitutional in *Danforth*. The women most affected by this law—those who most reasonably fear the consequences of notifying their husbands that they are pregnant—are in the gravest danger.

The husband's interest in the life of the child his wife is carrying does not permit the State to empower him with this troubling degree of authority over his wife. The contrary view leads to consequences reminiscent of the common law. A husband has no enforceable right to require a wife to advise him before she exercises her personal choices. If a husband's interest in the potential life of the child outweighs a wife's liberty, the State could require a married woman to notify her husband before she uses a postfertilization contraceptive. Perhaps next in line would be a statute requiring pregnant married women to notify their husbands before engaging in conduct causing risks to the fetus. After all, if the husband's interest in the fetus' safety is a sufficient predicate for state regulation, the State could reasonably conclude that pregnant wives should notify their husbands before drinking alcohol or smoking. Perhaps married women should notify their husbands before using contraceptives or before undergoing any type of surgery that may have complications affecting the husband's interest in his wife's reproductive organs. And if a husband's interest justifies notice in any of these cases, one might reasonably argue that it justifies exactly what the *Danforth* Court held it did not justify—a requirement of the husband's consent as well. A State may not give to a man the kind of dominion over his wife that parents exercise over their children. . . .

Our Constitution is a covenant running from the first generation of Americans to us and then to future generations. It is a coherent succession. Each generation must learn anew that the Constitution's written terms embody ideas and aspirations that must survive more ages than one. We accept our responsibility not to retreat from interpreting the full meaning of the covenant in light of all of our precedents. We invoke it once again to define the freedom guaranteed by the Constitution's own promise, the promise of liberty.

DISCUSSION QUESTIONS

1. In *Griswold v. Connecticut* seven justices split into three groups over why the Court had the authority to declare Connecticut's contraceptive control laws to be unconstitutional. Only one justice, Justice Clark, joined Justice Douglas's opinion, even though Chief Justice Warren had officially assigned the writing of the majority opinion to Justice Douglas. Yet, over the years that followed, it was Justice Douglas's words that later Courts cited to justify the existence of a right to privacy, not the opinions of Justice Goldberg, Harlan, or White. Why?

2. It has been argued that in the United States after the American Revolution every citizen enjoyed full rights before a new government was formed. Because of this, many legal scholars say it is reasonable to view the Bill of Rights in expansive terms as protecting broad individual rights. Do you agree with this view? Do you think this argument can be used to justify the right to obtain an abortion?

3. Some legal scholars believe Justices O'Connor, Kennedy, and Souter saved the legitimacy of the Supreme Court itself with their decision in *Planned Parenthood v. Casey*. Do you agree? What do you think would have happened if the Supreme Court had simply overturned *Roe v. Wade* in 1992 and abolished the constitutional right to obtain an abortion?

4. Critics argue that the idea of a constitutional right of privacy gives the Court too much power. Other scholars argue that there is a big difference between the general right of privacy and the view the Court took in the early decades of the twentieth century that any attempt to limit the power of private business was unconstitutional. What do you think?

CHAPTER
eight
✦ ✦ ✦ ✦ ✦ ✦ ✦ ✦

The Fourth Amendment Today

The Fourth Amendment was written, in the opinion of most Supreme Court justices who have been called upon to interpret it, to protect the private life of the people from unreasonable intrusions by government officials. The Court, from its first opinion interpreting the Fourth Amendment in 1886, refused to be tied to the specific words of the amendment. Those words gave very little guidance to the Court in deciding concrete legal cases. The amendment spoke of warrants but did not state when warrants were required. The amendment spoke of "persons, houses, papers, and effects," but surely other buildings besides "houses" and other things besides "papers and effects" were intended to be protected. The amendment spoke of "searches and seizures" but did not define what was meant by a search or how much control government had to exercise over things or people before they could be considered seized. From 1886 on, the Court assumed that the Fourth Amendment was intended to protect more than just property, and that privacy, the freedom to be left alone, was also included.

Beginning in 1914, the Court decided that the only way to enforce the Fourth Amendment's command that property and privacy be respected was to exclude from criminal trials evidence that had been obtained in violation of the Fourth Amendment. In 1961 the Court extended the exclusionary rule to state and local law enforcement after concluding that nothing else would force police at the local level to respect the commands of the Fourth Amendment. The fact that the exclusionary rule often meant that people convicted of terrible crimes would go free brought much public criticism to the Court, particularly the Warren Court. In no other area of constitutional law has the

Court been faced with such terrible decisions: enforce the Fourth Amendment and a convicted murderer goes free; don't enforce it and the Bill of Rights becomes meaningless.

During the 1960s the national media criticized the decisions of the Warren Court in this area, arguing that the police were "handcuffed" and the Court's decisions were "confused" and impossible to understand or apply. The criticism that the police were handcuffed was unfair. The Fourth Amendment handcuffed the police, not the Court. The criticism that the opinions of the Court were confusing and contradictory was more legitimate. As the years passed, more and more justices recognized that confusion did not help anyone and certainly did not insure that people's constitutional rights would be respected.

Part of the confusion sprang from the fact that even in the 1960s and 1970s American law was still trying to break free from the dictates of the ancient English common law in this area. Looking back on decisions handed down in the 1960s and 1970s, we may find it strange that the justices engaged in spirited debates about what the ancient English law might have been in 1776. Usually these debates provided much heat but very little light. Ultimately the Court moved the United States away from these ancient concepts and into the modern world. Police would no longer be prevented from searching for and seizing "mere evidence," whatever that was, and the fact that something was contraband, personal papers, or instrumentalities of crime would no longer have any effect on whether or not police could seize it.

From the beginning the Court recognized that the Fourth Amendment was intended to protect both property and privacy. At the same time it did not think the protection of property was coextensive with the law of trespass. Police could trespass on some private property, an open field for example, without violating the Fourth Amendment. Police could not trespass and violate the Fourth Amendment, however, such as by putting on a wiretap. The amendment protected some property interests and some privacy interests but not others.

In the 1960s the Court began to see the primary function of the Fourth Amendment as the protection of the reasonable expectation of privacy. The Court then had to decide which expectations of privacy it was willing to protect. People should not expect their backyards to be free from police observation from the air, for example, or their garbage to be free from police inspection. People should not expect that a field surrounded by fences and a "do not trespass" sign will be free from random police investigation.

As with other areas of constitutional law, the Court used a combination of balancing and line drawing to spell out the dictates of the Fourth Amendment. The Court balanced the property and privacy rights of the people against the legitimate needs of law enforcement. The Court divided the world into three areas: those that could only be searched with a warrant (except in emergencies); those that could be searched or seized with probable cause (with some exceptions); and those that could be searched without either probable cause or a warrant.

The question of when police need a warrant to search was very difficult for the Court. The Court began with the proposition that the police would usually need a warrant, and then over the years created so many exceptions that they seemed to swallow the rule. Today police generally only need a warrant if they wish to enter a private building, which means a home, including a hotel room, or the private area of a business. Areas open to the public, such as an open field or the showroom of a business, are not protected by the amendment.

The Court decided that seizing and searching people walking around in public places did not require a warrant, but in most cases police could only do so if they had probable cause. The extent to which police could seize and search automobiles caused much confusion as the Court struggled to come up with a rule that provided the right balance between the rights of individuals and the needs of modern law enforcement. Ultimately, the Court decided that a warrant would not be required before searching or seizing automobiles, or the containers found in automobiles.

Before a warrant can be issued or before police may search in most situations, probable cause is required. The concept of what exactly constitutes probable cause has changed over time. In the 1920s the fact that notorious bootleggers were driving a car from Detroit to Grand Rapids was enough to constitute probable cause. By the 1960s it was clear that more would be required before police could stop and search people on the open road. Generally police would need some reason to think this particular car contained contraband or evidence other than the fact that its drivers were generally known to be bad people. One of the problems that plagued police was the fluid nature of the probable cause concept. The Court tried to make this concept clearer by deciding concrete cases spelling out what was enough "cause" to make it "probable" that the car or person deserved to be searched or seized in each particular case.

Another difficult question for the Court was the extent to which police could be forced to reveal the name of informants who provided them with information. The Supreme Court accepted the notion that if police were forced to reveal the identity of their informants that would be the end of informants and much useful information would no longer be available to aid law enforcement. This made the whole process of deciding whether or not police actually had probable cause in concrete situations very difficult. Often probable cause consisted of information from a secret informant. It became almost impossible to know whether the police really had received such information or were making it up to justify their suspicions. Ultimately the Court had to accept the fact that there are limits to the amount of oversight the Court can have in these situations. It is up to states and cities to hire and train police officers who will respect the law and the Constitution they are sworn to uphold. It is up to judges at all levels to exercise their constitutional mandate to review police requests for warrants and not simply provide a rubber stamp whenever police have a suspicion.

The most legitimate criticism leveled against the Warren Court was that its decisions interpreting the Fourth Amendment were confusing. It is a criticism that could also be leveled against the Burger Court. After several years of decisions by the Rehnquist Court, much of the confusion has been eliminated. While people may object to where the Rehnquist Court has drawn the line in particular areas, the police and judges are no longer confused. It is fairly clear what the Fourth Amendment requires.

In the 1960s the Court expanded the concept of "privacy" it found in the Fourth Amendment to areas other than search and seizure. It came to the conclusion that the authors of the Bill of Rights did not intend the rights listed there be an exclusive list of all the rights enjoyed by Americans. A majority of justices came to accept Justice Brandeis's argument that "the makers of our Constitution undertook to secure conditions favorable to the pursuit of happiness" and that to accomplish this "they conferred, as against government, the right to be let alone—the most comprehensive of rights and the right most valued by civilized men."

In deciding on the limits of this right the Court concluded that people have a right to make fundamental decisions about their lives without unreasonable government interference and that this includes the right to decide whether or not to have an abortion. While the abortion issue proved difficult and divisive, ultimately a majority of justices confirmed that it was part of the right to privacy protected by the "emanations" flowing from the Bill of Rights.

Critics have argued that throughout the decades the Court has taken too expansive a view of its role in this area. The response has been that the Fourth Amendment outlaws "unreasonable" behavior on the part of government officials and only the Supreme Court, deciding concrete cases, can declare what is and what is not reasonable. Throughout the process the justices have been haunted by the descriptions by John Adams and others of the abuses of power that ultimately led to the American Revolution. While we assume that the American colonists in the 1700s objected to a lack of freedom of speech, they did not point to that as the cause of their rebellion. Rather, it was the specter of customs agents searching homes and warehouses without any justification that drove them to revolution. The colonists objected to having the privacy of their homes invaded by soldiers they were ordered to house and feed. Many invasions of privacy and dignity by government officials led to the shot heard round the world. It would be the specter of police searching the "sacred precincts of marital bedrooms for telltale signs of the use of contraceptives" that would lead Justice Douglas and the other justices to decide that the Bill of Rights protects the more general right of privacy.

Throughout the second half of the twentieth century another specter haunted the Court, that of George Orwell's Big Brother and the big brothers in charge of totalitarian states around the world. What is it that separates the United States from these regimes if it is not the right to "be let alone" and to live life free from unreasonable invasions by police and other government officials? At the same time, the Court has had to face the fact that the United States is a dangerous place. Any police officer walking down a dark alley knows that he or she may not come out alive. The dictates of the Fourth Amendment must accommodate the very real threat these officers face every day.

By the end of the twentieth century both the police and average citizens have a good idea of what the Fourth Amendment does and does not protect. While some of the rules may seem silly to some people, they are not confusing. From searching automobiles to backpacks to houses, mistakes can no longer be laid at the door of the Supreme Court. Police officers who violate the rules have only themselves to blame if a guilty person goes free because constitutional rights were violated.

The same is true of the more general right to privacy. While other areas may fall under its protection, we do know that people in the United States have the right to decide who they will marry, whether or not they will have children, and whether or not their children will attend private school. Women do have a right to control their own bodies, including the right to decide to have an abortion, limited only by the right states enjoy to regulate the abortion process to serve legitimate governmental goals.

In 1967 the national high school debate topic was whether or not Congress should write one uniform set of criminal procedure rules in the United States. While the U.S. Supreme Court has cleared up a lot of confusion about the meaning of the Fourth Amendment, it is important to realize that these decisions still do not constitute a uniform code of any sort. While the Supreme Court has decided what the Fourth Amendment of the United States Constitution requires, every state has a constitution interpreted by the state's supreme court. This means people in different states have rights beyond those recognized by the U.S. Supreme Court. In some states police need a warrant to search even though the Fourth Amendment does not require one. Given that every citizen is protected by two sets of rights, one federal and one state, there can never be a uniform code of criminal procedure.

At the same time the Supreme Court's interpretations of the Fourth Amendment to the Constitution apply to everyone and have provided guidance as to how similar provisions in state constitutions should be interpreted. It is the Fourth Amendment that protects everyone from unreasonable searches and seizures and it is the Bill of Rights that protects everyone's general right to privacy, a right that has proved to be both comprehensive and controversial.

GLOSSARY OF LEGAL TERMS

❋ ❋ ❋ ❋ ❋ ❋ ❋ ❋

A fortiori: Latin, meaning literally "from the stronger." It is used by judges to mean that if one fact exists, another fact must follow from it. If someone is alive, then we know *a fortiori* that he or she is breathing.

Allegation: A statement of fact that has not yet been proven. In a criminal case we would say that allegations have been made against the defendant which the prosecutor will attempt to prove.

Amicus curiae: Latin, meaning literally "a friend of the Court." In some cases, especially in cases that have been appealed, other people besides those people directly involved in a case may have an interest in the outcome. In an effort to influence the justices, these people will file briefs as "friends of the Court," suggesting why the decision should come out one way or the other. When people file *amicus curiae* briefs, they are usually arguing that the court's decision will have an impact on them or on society in general which the court should consider when making its decision.

Analogy: A way of thinking about an issue that relates a particular situation to another situation by identifying similarities. People involved in a case often argue that their case is analogous (or similar) to another case because they know what the court decided in the other case and they would like the court to make the same decision in their case.

Appeal: A request to a higher court to review the decision of a lower court. When a trial is over, the losing party may appeal the decision to an appeals court.

Appellant/Appellee: The appellant is the person who appeals a case to a higher court; the appellee is the person who has to respond to the appeal.

Atheist: A person who does not believe in the existence of a God.

Bill of attainder: A law passed by a legislature declaring that a particular person or a group of persons is guilty of a crime. The person, or group of persons, to whom the bill of attainder applies has not received a trial.

Brief: A written document given to a judge to support a particular legal opinion. When a case is appealed to a higher court, each side will file a brief explaining why it should win the case. Other people may also file briefs as "friends of the Court" (*amicus curiae* briefs), pointing out the effects a decision may have on them or on society in general.

Certiorari: Latin, meaning literally "to be certain." In American law, when someone wants to appeal his or her case to the U.S. Supreme Court, he or she usually asks for a writ of certiorari. If the Court agrees to hear the case, it issues a writ of certiorari which orders the parties in the case to bring the case before the court.

Circuit Court of Appeals: In the federal judicial system, the district court conducts the trial and the Supreme Court hears cases on appeal. There is an appeals court between the district court and the Supreme Court, called the circuit court. Generally a case must be appealed to the circuit court before it can go on to the Supreme Court.

Citizen: Someone who is a full legal member of a nation. In the United States, only a citizen can vote and hold some public offices.

Civil: In American law, most cases are either civil or criminal. In a civil case, one person sues another person. In a criminal case, the government claims that someone has broken the law and should pay a fine or go to jail.

Common law: Common law is law made by judges as opposed to statutes passed by legislatures. In ancient times, people were subject to the laws of their tribe. After his conquest of England in 1066 A.D., William I decided that there should be one law for all of the subjects in his kingdom. This law was developed mainly by the king's judges, as they made decisions and then based later decisions on their decisions in earlier cases. Over the centuries the English judges developed many legal principles that became the basis for most of their decisions in civil cases. These principles became the common law for England and her colonies. The United States inherited this common law. It has been modified by the judges in each state over the centuries, so that today each state is considered to have its own unique common law. The main exception to this is Louisiana, which bases its law on French and Spanish law, not the English common law.

Conscientious objector: A person who, for reasons of conscience, objects to fighting in a war. To qualify as a true "conscientious objector," the person must believe that war is objectionable in general, and not just object to a particular war.

Constitution: In the United States, the Constitution is a written document that forms the supreme law and organization of the government. Governments may exercise only those powers granted to them by the Constitution and they are limited by the rights reserved for the individual citizens.

Criminal: *See* **Civil.**

De minimis: The short form of the Latin phrase *de minimis non curat lex*, which means the law does not care about very "minimal" or small things. If a legal violation is technically a violation of the law but so small as to be not worth the court's time, the judge may dismiss the case as *de minimis*.

Defendant: A defendant is someone who is being sued or is charged with committing a crime.

Dicta: From the Latin, meaning statements of opinion by a judge that are not directly relevant to the decision of the case. Dicta are general statements concerning a particular judge's definition of the law but that do not directly relate to the case before the court.

Dissent: When a group of judges is making a decision and some of the judges do not agree with the majority, they will "dissent" from the majority opinion. To dissent simply means to disagree. They may state their dissent, or they may write a dissenting opinion explaining why they disagree. On some occasions a dissenting opinion has convinced the group to reverse its opinion about a decision.

District court: In the federal judicial system, trial of a case is held at the district court. A case may then be appealed to the circuit court, and from there to the Supreme Court. It is the district court that determines the facts of the case.

Ex post facto law: A law passed after an act has been committed. Conviction on the basis of an ex post facto law is not allowed in the United States; a person may only be convicted of acts for which laws were actually on the books when the act was committed.

Holding: The decision of the court and the reason for that decision. Attorneys generally say that the holding of the case is the reason why the winning party in a case was successful.

Impeachment: Impeachment occurs when a public official is removed from office for having done something illegal or immoral.

In loco parentis: Latin, meaning literally "in the place of the parent." *In loco parentis* is a legal concept that says that if someone, such as a babysitter or a teacher, has been put in charge of a child, then that person has the same power over the child that the child's parent would have.

Infra: Latin, meaning literally "below." If a judge mentions a case briefly that he or she will be discussing in detail later in the decision, then the judge may put the word *infra* after the name of the case. This lets the reader know that the case will be discussed later in more detail.

Injunction: A court order telling a person to do, or not to do, something. People might say that a person has been "injoined" from acting. A restraining order is one kind of injunction.

Interstate commerce: The movement of goods across state lines in the United States. Under the U.S. Constitution, the federal government is given the power to control "interstate commerce" to make sure that goods flow between states with a minimum of disruption.

Jurisdiction: The area over which a particular court has power. For example, the U.S. Supreme Court can only decide cases concerned with federal law and questions of constitutional interpretation. Most issues are within the jurisdiction of state courts, not federal courts.

Mens rea: Latin, meaning literally "guilty mind." Generally, a person cannot be found guilty of a crime unless he or she had a "guilty mind," meaning he or she intended to do harm or to commit a crime.

Naturalization: The process by which a noncitizen becomes a citizen.

Parens patriae: Latin, meaning literally "the parent of the country." In ancient times this term meant that the king was regarded as the ultimate parent for everyone and had the power to act as the parent of any subject in the kingdom if the subject's real parents were not available. In countries without a king, the term means that, if there is no natural parent to deal with a problem, then the government may have to fulfill that function. For example, the government may act as a parent in dealing with a child, with an insane person, or with someone who is not capable of dealing with things for himself or herself.

Per curiam: Latin, meaning literally "by the court." When an opinion has been written by the court as a whole, rather than by one particular judge, it is called a *per curiam* decision.

Petitioner: A person who petitions a judge to make a decision. Someone who files a lawsuit or begins an appeal can be called a petitioner. The person who is being sued or is defending against an appeal is the respondent.

Plaintiff: In a lawsuit, the person who brings the lawsuit is called the plaintiff. The person being sued by the plaintiff is called the defendant. The defendant defends against the charges that have been brought by the plaintiff.

Police power: A concept of U.S. law. Courts in the United States have decided that state constitutions provide state governments with police power, meaning the power to do everything that it is "reasonable" for government to do. Although the U.S. Constitution spells out the powers of the federal government, most state constitutions do not do this. The police power is very broad and includes the power to build roads, fight disease, and put people in jail; however, a court can decide that a particular action by a state legislature is unconstitutional if it is beyond the police power. The problem with this broad concept is that it is very vague and gives courts a great deal of power to declare the actions of legislatures to be unconstitutional as a violation of the state constitution. If a state government takes action beyond its power, the court does not have to ask whether or not any rights protected by the Bill of Rights have been violated. A court may invalidate an action of government either because the action was beyond the power of government or because it violated a right protected by the Bill of Rights.

Precedent: In the U.S. legal system, lower courts are bound by the decisions of courts above them. We say that those higher court decisions serve as precedents for the decisions to be made by the lower courts.

Restraining order: A court order that orders someone not to do something. If a person wants to stop another person from doing something, he or she may ask a judge for a restraining order against that other person.

Scienter: Latin, meaning "knowingly." Generally people cannot be convicted of crimes unless they acted knowingly, with scienter, meaning that the people knew what they were doing when they committed the crime. They were not acting unconsciously or without knowledge of the facts in the case.

Separation of powers: Generally government is thought of as having three basic powers: the power to make the law (legislative), the power to enforce the law (executive), and the power to decide what the law is (judicial). In the

United States, these three powers are separate from each other. That has not always been true in other countries or in the past. In ancient Athens, for example, the legislature was also the supreme court.

Standing: In the American legal system, people are generally not allowed to complain about a violation of the law or the Constitution unless the violation has injured them personally in some way. Only people who actually have been injured have standing to complain about their injury in a civil or criminal case.

Stare decisis: Latin, meaning literally "the decision must stand." In American law, once a particular court has made a decision, it is expected that the court will not change its ruling. People can then alter their behavior to comply with the decision without fear that it will change in the near future. This concept is particularly important for the U.S. Supreme Court because Supreme Court decisions have such a far-reaching impact on society.

Statute: A law passed by a legislative body, such as a state legislature or the U.S. Congress.

Stipulate: The purpose of a trial is to determine the facts of a particular case. If there are facts on which both sides agree, then both sides will "stipulate" that those facts are true and correct. For the rest of the trial, everyone will assume that those facts are true without having to prove them.

Supra: Latin, meaning literally "above." If a judge has already discussed a case in detail and wishes to mention it briefly again, he or she may put the word *supra* after the name of the case to let the reader know that the case has already been discussed in detail earlier in the decision.

Tort: Comes from the same Latin root as words such as *twist* and *torture.* In American law, if one person has injured another person in some way, we say that a tort has been committed. The injury may be physical, economic, or psychological. When people sue because they have been injured, we say they are "suing in tort."

Ubiquity: The concept that something can be everywhere at the same time, omnipresent. Some believe that God is ubiquitous. We generally conceive that the law and government are ubiquitous, even if there is no government official at a particular place at a particular time.

Writ of habeas corpus: A court order that requires a person who has someone under custody to either bring that person to court or release him or her from custody.

FURTHER READING

* * * * * * * *

Franklin, Paula A. *The Fourth Amendment*. Morristown, NJ: Silver Burdett Press, 1991.
 Explains search and seizure law in a way that is accessible to children.

Hixon, Richard. *Privacy in a Public Society*. Oxford: Oxford University Press, 1987.
 Examines the conflict between the desire to protect privacy and the need to protect the right of free speech and press.

LaFave, Wayne R. *Search and Seizure*. St. Paul, MN: West Publishing Co., 1987.
 A four-volume treatise, written for attorneys, that explores the Fourth Amendment.

Landynski, Jacob W. *Search and Seizure and the Supreme Court*. Baltimore, MD: Johns Hopkins Press, 1966.
 A study of the law of search and seizure.

Lapidus, Edith J. *Eavesdropping on Trial*. Rochelle Park, NJ: Hayden Book Co., 1974.
 Discusses the law concerning electronic eavesdropping.

Ringel, William F. *Searches & Seizures, Arrests and Confessions*. New York: Clark, Boardman, Callaghan, 1993.
 A three-volume treatise, written for attorneys, on the law of searches, arrests, and confessions.

Schwartz, Herman, ed. *The Burger Years*. New York: Viking, 1987.
 A collection of articles about the decisions handed down while Warren Burger was chief justice of the Supreme Court.

Tribe, Laurence. *The Clash of Absolutes*. New York: W.W. Norton & Co., 1990.
 Discusses the constitutional right to privacy and the right to have an abortion.

Vandiver, James U. *Criminal Investigation*. Metuchen, NJ: Scarecrow Press, 1983.
    Discusses the laws that control the criminal investigation process.

Zare, Melvyn. *The Bill of Rights and the Police*. Dobbs Ferry, NY: Oceana, 1980.
    Examines the rights contained in the Bill of Rights that are relevant to police
    investigations, including the Fourth Amendment.

APPENDIX
A

* * * * * * * * *

Constitution of the United States

PREAMBLE

We the People of the United States, in Order to form a more perfect Union, establish Justice, insure domestic Tranquility, provide for the common defence, promote the general Welfare, and secure the Blessings of Liberty to ourselves and our Posterity, do ordain and establish this Constitution for the United States of America.

ARTICLE I

Section 1. All legislative Powers herein granted shall be vested in a Congress of the United States, which shall consist of a Senate and House of Representatives.

Section 2. The House of Representatives shall be composed of Members chosen every second Year by the People of the several States, and the Electors in each State shall have the Qualifications requisite for Electors of the most numerous Branch of the State Legislature.

No Person shall be a Representative who shall not have attained to the age of twenty five Years, and been seven Years a Citizen of the United States, and who shall not, when elected, be an Inhabitant of that State in which he shall be chosen.

Representatives and direct Taxes shall be apportioned among the several States which may be included within this Union, according to their respective Numbers, which shall be determined by adding to the whole Number of free Persons, including those bound to Service for a Term of Years, and excluding Indians not taxed, three fifths of all other Persons. The actual

Enumeration shall be made within three Years after the first Meeting of the Congress of the United States, and within every subsequent Term of ten Years, in such Manner as they shall by Law direct. The Number of Representatives shall not exceed one for every thirty Thousand, but each State shall have at Least one Representative; and until such enumeration shall be made, the State of New Hampshire shall be entitled to chuse three, Massachusetts eight, Rhode-Island and Providence Plantations one, Connecticut five, New-York six, New Jersey four, Pennsylvania eight, Delaware one, Maryland six, Virginia ten, North Carolina five, South Carolina five, and Georgia three.

When vacancies happen in the Representation from any State, the Executive Authority thereof shall issue Writs of Election to fill such Vacancies.

The House of Representatives shall chuse their Speaker and other Officers; and shall have the sole Power of Impeachment.

Section 3. The Senate of the United States shall be composed of two Senators from each State, chosen by the Legislature thereof, for six Years; and each Senator shall have one Vote.

Immediately after they shall be assembled in Consequence of the first Election, they shall be divided as equally as may be into three Classes. The Seats of the Senators of the first Class shall be vacated at the Expiration of the second Year, of the second Class at the Expiration of the fourth Year, and of the third Class at the Expiration of the sixth Year, so that one third may be chosen every second Year; and if Vacancies happen by Resignation, or otherwise, during the Recess of the Legislature of any State, the Executive thereof may make temporary Appointments until the next Meeting of the Legislature, which shall then fill such Vacancies.

No Person shall be a Senator who shall not have attained to the Age of thirty Years, and been nine Years a Citizen of the United States, and who shall not, when elected, be an Inhabitant of that State for which he shall be chosen.

The Vice President of the United States shall be President of the Senate, but shall have no Vote, unless they be equally divided.

The Senate shall chuse their other Officers, and also a President pro tempore, in the Absence of the Vice President, or when he shall exercise the Office of President of the United States.

The Senate shall have the sole Power to try all Impeachments. When sitting for that Purpose, they shall be on Oath or Affirmation. When the President of the United States is tried the Chief Justice shall preside: And no Person shall be convicted without the Concurrence of two thirds of the Members present.

Judgment in Cases of Impeachment shall not extend further than to removal from Office, and disqualification to hold and enjoy any Office of honor, Trust or Profit under the United States: but the Party convicted shall nevertheless be liable and subject to Indictment, Trial, Judgment and Punishment, according to Law.

Section 4. The Times, Places and Manner of holding Elections for Senators and Representatives, shall be prescribed in each State by the Legislature thereof; but the Congress may at any time by Law make or alter such Regulations, except as to the Places of chusing Senators.

The Congress shall assemble at least once in every Year, and such Meeting shall be on the first Monday in December, unless they shall by Law appoint a different Day.

Section 5. Each House shall be the Judge of the Elections, Returns and Qualifications of its own Members, and a Majority of each shall constitute a Quorum to do Business; but a smaller Number may adjourn from day to day, and may be authorized to compel the Attendance of absent Members, in such Manner, and under such Penalties as each House may provide.

Each House may determine the Rules of its Proceedings, punish its Members for disorderly Behaviour, and, with the Concurrence of two thirds, expel a Member.

Each House shall keep a Journal of its Proceedings, and from time to time publish the same, excepting such Parts as may in their Judgment require Secrecy; and the Yeas and Nays of the Members of either House on any question shall, at the Desire of one fifth of those Present, be entered on the Journal.

Neither House, during the Session of Congress, shall, without the Consent of the other, adjourn for more than three days, nor to any other Place than that in which the two Houses shall be sitting.

Section 6. The Senators and Representatives shall receive a Compensation for their Services, to be ascertained by Law, and paid out of the Treasury of the United States. They shall in all Cases, except Treason, Felony and Breach of the Peace, be privileged from Arrest during their Attendance at the Session of their respective Houses, and in going to and returning from the same; and for any Speech or Debate in either House, they shall not be questioned in any other Place.

No Senator or Representative shall, during the Time for which he was elected, be appointed to any civil Office under the Authority of the United States, which shall have been created, or the Emoluments whereof shall have been encreased during such time; and no Person holding any Office under the United States, shall be a Member of either House during his Continuance in Office.

Section 7. All Bills for raising Revenue shall originate in the House of Representatives; but the Senate may propose or concur with amendments as on other Bills.

Every Bill which shall have passed the House of Representatives and the Senate, shall, before it become a Law, be presented to the President of the United States; If he approve he shall sign it, but if not he shall return it, with his Objections to that House in which it shall have originated, who shall enter the Objections at large on their Journal, and proceed to reconsider it. If after such Reconsideration two thirds of that House shall agree to pass the Bill, it shall be sent, together with the Objections, to the other House, by which it shall likewise be reconsidered, and if approved by two thirds of that House, it shall become a Law. But in all such Cases the Votes of both Houses shall be determined by yeas and Nays, and the Names of the Persons voting for and against the Bill shall be entered on the Journal of each House respectively. If any Bill shall not be returned by the President within ten Days (Sunday excepted) after it shall have been presented to him, the Same shall be a Law, in like Manner as if he had signed it, unless the Congress by their Adjournment prevent its Return, in which Case it shall not be a Law.

Every Order, Resolution, or Vote to which the Concurrence of the Senate and House of Representatives may be necessary (except on a question of Adjournment) shall be presented to the President of the United States; and before the Same shall take Effect, shall be approved by him, or being disapproved by him, shall be repassed by two thirds of the Senate and House of Representatives, according to the Rules and Limitations prescribed in the Case of a Bill.

Section 8. The Congress shall have Power To lay and collect Taxes, Duties, Imposts and Excises, to pay the Debts and provide for the common Defence and general Welfare of the United States; but all Duties, Imposts and Excises shall be uniform throughout the United States;

To borrow Money on the credit of the United States;

To regulate Commerce with foreign Nations, and among the several States, and with the Indian Tribes;

To establish an uniform Rule of Naturalization, and uniform Laws on the subject of Bankruptcies throughout the United States;

To coin Money, regulate the Value thereof, and of foreign Coin, and fix the Standard of Weights and Measures;

To provide for the Punishment of counterfeiting the Securities and current Coin of the United States;

To establish Post Offices and post Roads;

To promote the Progress of Science and useful Arts, by securing for limited Times to Authors and Inventors the exclusive Right to their respective Writings and Discoveries;

To constitute Tribunals inferior to the supreme Court;

To define and punish Piracies and Felonies commit[t]ed on the high Seas, and Offences against the Law of Nations;

To declare War, grant Letters of Marque and Reprisal, and make Rules concerning Captures on Land and Water;

To raise and support Armies, but no Appropriation of Money to that Use shall be for a longer Term than two Years;

To provide and maintain a Navy;

To make Rules for the Government and Regulation of the land and naval Forces;

To provide for calling forth the Militia to execute the Laws of the Union, suppress Insurrections and repel Invasions;

To provide for organizing, arming, and disciplining the Militia, and for governing such Part of them as may be employed in the Service of the United States, reserving to the States respectively, the Appointment of the Officers, and the Authority of training the Militia according to the discipline pre-scribed by Congress;

To exercise exclusive Legislation in all Cases whatsoever, over such District (not exceeding ten Miles square) as may, by Cession of Particular States, and the Acceptance of Congress, become the Seat of the Govern-ment of the United States, and to exercise like Authority over all Places purchased by the Consent of the Legislature of the State in which the Same shall be, for the Erection of Forts, Magazines, Arsenals, dock-Yards, and other needful Buildings;

—And

To make all Laws which shall be necessary and proper for carrying into Execution the foregoing Powers, and all other Powers vested by this Consti-tution in the Government of the United States, or in any Department or Officer thereof.

Section 9. The Migration or Importation of such Persons as any of the States now existing shall think proper to admit, shall not be prohibited by the Congress prior to the Year one thousand eight hundred and eight, but a Tax or duty may be imposed on such Importation, not exceeding ten dollars for each Person.

The Privilege of the Writ of Habeas Corpus shall not be suspended, unless when in Cases of Rebellion or Invasion the public Safety may require it.

No Bill of Attainder or ex post facto Law shall be passed.

No capitation, or other direct, Tax shall be laid, unless in Proportion to the Census or Enumeration herein before directed to be taken.

No Tax or Duty shall be laid on Articles exported from any State.

No Preference shall be given by any Regulation of Commerce or Revenue to the Ports of one State over those of another; nor shall Vessels bound to, or from, one State, be obliged to enter, clear or pay Duties in another.

No Money shall be drawn from the Treasury, but in Consequence of Appropriations made by Law; and a regular Statement and Account of the Receipts and Expenditures of all public Money shall be published from time to time.

No Title of Nobility shall be granted by the United States: And no Person holding any Office of Profit or Trust under them, shall, without the Consent of the Congress, accept of any present, Emolument, Office, or Title, of any kind whatever, from any King, Prince or foreign State.

Section 10. No State shall enter into any Treaty, Alliance, or Confederation; grant Letters of Marque and Reprisal; coin Money; emit Bills of Credit; make any Thing but gold and silver Coin a Tender in Payment of Debts; pass any Bill of Attainder, ex post facto Law, or Law impairing the Obligation of Contracts, or grant any Title of Nobility.

No State shall, without the Consent of the Congress, lay any Imposts or Duties on Imports or Exports, except what may be absolutely necessary for executing it's inspection Laws: and the net Produce of all Duties and Imposts, laid by any State on Imports or Exports, shall be for the Use of the Treasury of the United States; and all such Laws shall be subject to the Revision and Controul of the Congress.

No State shall, without the Consent of Congress, lay any Duty of Tonnage, keep Troops, or Ships of War in time of Peace, enter into any Agreement or Compact with another State, or with a foreign Power, or engage in War, unless actually invaded, or in such imminent Danger as will not admit of delay.

ARTICLE II

Section 1. The executive Power shall be vested in a President of the United States of America. He shall hold his Office during the Term of four Years, and, together with the Vice President, chosen for the same Term, be elected, as follows.

Each State shall appoint, in such Manner as the Legislature thereof may direct, a Number of Electors, equal to the whole Number of Senators and Representatives to which the State may be entitled in the Congress: but no Senator or Representative, or Person holding an Office of Trust or Profit under the United States, shall be appointed an Elector.

The Electors shall meet in their respective States, and vote by Ballot for two Persons, of whom one at least shall not be an Inhabitant of the same State with themselves. And they shall make a List of all the Persons voted for, and of the Number of Votes for each; which List they shall sign and certify, and transmit sealed to the Seat of the Government of the United States, directed to the President of the Senate. The President of the Senate shall, in the Presence of the Senate and House of Representatives, open all the Certificates, and the Votes shall then be counted. The Person having the greatest Number of Votes shall be the President, if such Number be a Majority of the whole Number of Electors appointed; and if there be more than one who have such Majority, and have an equal Number of Votes, then the House of Representatives shall immediately chuse by Ballot one of them for President; and if no Person have a Majority, then from the five highest on the list the said House shall in like Manner chuse the President. But in chusing the President, the Votes shall be taken by States, the Representation from each State having one Vote; a quorum for this Purpose shall consist of a Member or Members from two thirds of the States, and a Majority of all the States shall be necessary to a Choice. In every Case, after the Choice of the President, the Person having the greatest Number of Votes of the Electors shall be the Vice President. But if there should remain two or more who have equal Votes, the Senate shall chuse from them by Ballot the Vice President.

The Congress may determine the Time of chusing the Electors, and the Day on which they shall give their Votes; which Day shall be the same throughout the United States.

No Person except a natural born Citizen, or a Citizen of the United States, at the time of the Adoption of this Constitution, shall be eligible to the Office of President; neither shall any Person be eligible to that Office who shall not have attained to the Age of thirty five Years, and been fourteen Years a Resident within the United States.

In Case of the Removal of the President from Office, or of his Death, Resignation, or Inability to discharge the Powers and Duties of the said Office, the Same shall devolve on the Vice President, and the Congress may by Law provide for the Case of Removal, Death, Resignation or Inability, both of the President and Vice President, declaring what Officer shall then act as President, and such Officer shall act accordingly, until the Disability be removed, or a President shall be elected.

The President shall, at stated Times, receive for his Services, a Compensation, which shall neither be encreased nor diminished during the Period for which he shall have been elected, and he shall not receive within that Period any other Emolument from the United States, or any of them.

Before he enter on the Execution of his Office, he shall take the following Oath or Affirmation:—"I do solemnly swear (or affirm) that I will faithfully execute the Office of President of the United States, and will to the best of my Ability, preserve, protect and defend the Constitution of the United States."

Section 2. The President shall be Commander in Chief of the Army and Navy of the United States, and of the Militia of the several States, when called into the actual Service of the United States; he may require the Opinion, in writing, of the principal Officer in each of the executive Departments, upon any Subject relating to the Duties of their respective Offices, and he shall have Power to grant Reprieves and Pardons for Offenses against the United States, except in Cases of Impeachment.

He shall have Power, by and with the Advice and Consent of the Senate, to make Treaties, provided two thirds of the Senators present concur; and he shall nominate, and by and with the Advice and Consent of the Senate, shall appoint Ambassadors, other public Ministers and Consuls, Judges of the supreme Court, and all other Officers of the United States, whose Appointments are not herein otherwise provided for, and which shall be established by Law: but the Congress may by Law vest the Appointment of such inferior Officers, as they think proper, in the President alone, in the Courts of Law, or in the Heads of Departments.

The President shall have Power to fill up all Vacancies that may happen during the Recess of the Senate, by granting Commissions which shall expire at the End of their next Session.

Section 3. He shall from time to time give to the Congress Information of the State of the Union, and recommend to their Consideration such Measures as he shall judge necessary and expedient; he may, on extraordinary Occasions, convene both Houses, or either of them, and in Case of Disagreement between them, with Respect to the Time of Adjournment, he may adjourn them to such Time as he shall think proper; he shall receive Ambassadors and other public Ministers; he shall take Care that the Laws be faithfully executed, and shall Commission all the Officers of the United States.

Section 4. The President, Vice President and all Civil Officers of the United States, shall be removed from office on Impeachment for, and Conviction of, Treason, Bribery, or other high Crimes and Misdemeanors.

ARTICLE III

Section 1. The judicial Power of the United States shall be vested in one supreme Court, and in such inferior Courts as the Congress may from time to time ordain and establish. The Judges, both of the supreme and inferior Courts, shall hold their Offices during good Behaviour, and shall, at stated

Times, receive for their Services, a Compensation, which shall not be diminished during their Continuance in Office.

Section 2. The judicial Power shall extend to all Cases, in Law and Equity, arising under this Constitution, the Laws of the United States, and Treaties made, or which shall be made, under their Authority;—to all Cases affecting Ambassadors, other public Ministers and Consuls;—to all Cases of admiralty and maritime Jurisdiction;—to Controversies to which the United States shall be a Party;—to Controversies between two or more States;—between a State and Citizens of another State;—between Citizens of different States;—between Citizens of the same State claiming Lands under Grants of different States, and between a State, or the Citizens thereof, and foreign States, Citizens or Subjects.

In all Cases affecting Ambassadors, other public Ministers and Consuls, and those in which a State shall be Party, the supreme Court shall have original Jurisdiction. In all the other Cases before mentioned, the supreme Court shall have appellate Jurisdiction, both as to Law and Fact, with such Exceptions, and under such Regulations as the Congress shall make.

The Trial of all Crimes, except in cases of Impeachment, shall be by Jury; and such Trial shall be held in the State where the said Crimes shall have been committed; but when not committed within any State, the Trial shall be at such Place or Places as the Congress may by Law have directed.

Section 3. Treason against the United States shall consist only in levying War against them, or in adhering to their Enemies, giving them Aid and Comfort. No Person shall be convicted of Treason unless on the Testimony of two Witnesses to the same overt Act, or on Confession in open Court.

The Congress shall have Power to declare the Punishment of Treason, but no Attainder of Treason shall work Corruption of Blood, or Forfeiture except during the Life of the Person attainted.

ARTICLE IV

Section 1. Full Faith and Credit shall be given in each State to the public Acts, Records, and judicial Proceedings of every other State. And the Congress may by general Laws prescribe the Manner in which such Acts, Records and Proceedings shall be proved, and the Effect thereof.

Section 2. The Citizens of each State shall be entitled to all Privileges and Immunities of Citizens in the several States.

A Person charged in any State with Treason, Felony, or other Crime, who shall flee from Justice, and be found in another State, shall on Demand of the executive Authority of the State from which he fled, be delivered up, to be removed to the State having Jurisdiction of the Crime.

No Person held to Service or Labour in one State, under the Laws thereof, escaping into another, shall, in Consequence of any Law or Regulation therein, be discharged from such Service or Labour, but shall be delivered up on Claim of the Party to whom such Service or Labour may be due.

Section 3. New States may be admitted by the Congress into this Union; but no new State shall be formed or erected within the Jurisdiction of any other State; nor any State be formed by the Junction of two or more States, or Parts of States, without the Consent of the Legislatures of the States concerned as well as of the Congress.

The Congress shall have Power to dispose of and make all needful Rules and Regulations respecting the Territory or other Property belonging to the United States; and nothing in this Constitution shall be so construed as to Prejudice any Claims of the United States, or of any particular State.

Section 4. The United States shall guarantee to every State in this Union a Republican Form of Government, and shall protect each of them against invasion; and on Application of the Legislature, or of the Executive (when the Legislature cannot be convened) against domestic Violence.

ARTICLE V

The Congress, whenever two thirds of both Houses shall deem it necessary, shall propose Amendments to this Constitution, or, on the Application of the Legislatures of two thirds of the several States, shall call a Convention for proposing Amendments, which, in either Case, shall be valid to all Intents and Purposes, as Part of this Constitution, when ratified by the Legislatures of three fourths of the several States, or by Conventions in three fourths thereof, as the one or the other Mode of Ratification may be proposed by the Congress; Provided that no Amendment which may be made prior to the Year One thousand eight hundred and eight shall in any Manner affect the first and fourth Clauses in the Ninth Section of the first Article; and that no State, without its Consent, shall be deprived of its equal Suffrage in the Senate.

ARTICLE VI

All Debts contracted and Engagements entered into, before the Adoption of this Constitution, shall be as valid against the United States under this Constitution, as under the Confederation.

This Constitution, and the Laws of the United States which shall be made in Pursuance thereof; and all Treaties made, or which shall be made, under the Authority of the United States, shall be the supreme Law of the Land; and the Judges in every State shall be the supreme Law of the Land; and the

Judges in every State shall be bound thereby, any Thing in the Constitution or Laws of any State to the Contrary notwithstanding.

The Senators and Representatives before mentioned, and the Members of the several State Legislatures, and all executive and judicial Officers, both of the United States and of the several States, shall be bound by Oath or Affirmation, to support this Constitution; but no religious Test shall ever be required as a Qualification to any Office or public Trust under the United States.

ARTICLE VII

The Ratification of the Conventions of nine States, shall be sufficient for the Establishment of this Constitution between the States so ratifying the Same.

AMENDMENTS
Amendment I

Congress shall make no law respecting an establishment of religion, or prohibiting the free exercise thereof; or abridging the freedom of speech, or of the press; or the right of the people peaceably to assemble, and to petition the Government for a redress of grievances.

Amendment II

A well regulated Militia, being necessary to the security of a free State, the right of the people to keep and bear Arms, shall not be infringed.

Amendment III

No Soldier shall, in time of peace be quartered in any house, without the consent of the Owner, nor in time of war, but in a manner to be prescribed by law.

Amendment IV

The right of the people to be secure in their persons, houses, papers, and effects, against unreasonable searches and seizures, shall not be violated, and no Warrants shall issue, but upon probable cause, supported by Oath or affirmation, and particularly describing the place to be searched, and the persons or things to be seized.

Amendment V

No person shall be held to answer for a capital, or otherwise infamous crime, unless on a presentment or indictment of a Grand Jury, except in cases arising in the land or naval forces, or in the Militia, when in actual service in time of War or public danger; nor shall any person be subject for the same offence to be twice put in jeopardy of life or limb; nor shall be compelled in any criminal case to be a witness against himself, nor be deprived of life, liberty, or property, without due process of law; nor shall private property be taken for public use, without just compensation.

Amendment VI

In all criminal prosecutions, the accused shall enjoy the right to a speedy and public trial, by an impartial jury of the State and district wherein the crime shall have been committed, which district shall have been previously ascertained by law, and to be informed of the nature and cause of the accusation; to be confronted with the witnesses against him; to have compulsory process for obtaining witnesses in his favor, and to have the Assistance of Counsel for his defence.

Amendment VII

In Suits at common law, where the value in controversy shall exceed twenty dollars, the right of trial by jury shall be preserved, and no fact tried by a jury, shall be otherwise re-examined in any Court of the United States, than according to the rules of the common law.

Amendment VIII

Excessive bail shall not be required, nor excessive fines imposed, nor cruel and unusual punishments inflicted.

Amendment IX

The enumeration in the Constitution, of certain rights, shall not be construed to deny or disparage others retained by the people.

Amendment X

The powers not delegated to the United States by the Constitution, nor prohibited by it to the States, are reserved to the States respectively, or to the people.

[First 10 amendments ratified 15 December 1791]

Amendment XI

The Judicial power of the United States shall not be construed to extend to any suit in law or equity, commenced or prosecuted against one of the United States by Citizens of another State, or by Citizens or Subjects of any Foreign State.

[Ratified 7 February 1795]

Amendment XII

The Electors shall meet in their respective states and vote by ballot for President and Vice-President, one of whom, at least, shall not be an inhabitant of the same state with themselves; they shall name in their ballots the person voted for as President, and in distinct ballots the person voted for as Vice-President, and they shall make distinct lists of all persons voted for as President, and of all persons voted for as Vice-President, and of the number of votes for each, which lists they shall sign and certify, and transmit sealed to the seat of the government of the United States, directed to the President of the Senate;—The President of the Senate shall, in the presence of the Senate and House of Representatives, open all the certificates and the votes shall then be counted;—The person having the greatest number of votes for President, shall be the President, if such number be a majority of the whole number of Electors appointed; and if no person have such majority, then from the persons having the highest numbers not exceeding three on the list of those voted for as President, the House of Representatives shall chuse immediately, by ballot, the President. But in chusing the President, the votes shall be taken by states, the representation from each state having one vote; a quorum for this purpose shall consist of a member or members from two-thirds of the states, and a majority of all the states shall be necessary to a choice. And if the House of Representatives shall not chuse a President whenever the right of choice shall devolve upon them, before the fourth day of March next following, then the Vice-President shall act as President, as in the case of the death or other constitutional disability of the President—The person having the greatest number of votes as Vice-President, shall be the Vice-President, if such number be a majority of the whole number of Electors appointed, and if no person have a majority, then from the two highest numbers on the list, the Senate shall chuse the Vice-President; a quorum for the purpose shall consist of two-thirds of the whole number of Senators, and a majority of the whole number shall be necessary to a choice. But no person constitutionally ineligible to the office of President shall be eligible to that of Vice-President of the United States.

[Ratified 27 July 1804]

Amendment XIII

Section 1. Neither slavery nor involuntary servitude, except as a punishment for crime whereof the party shall have been duly convicted, shall exist within the United States, or any place subject to their jurisdiction.

Section 2. Congress shall have power to enforce this article by appropriate legislation.

[Ratified 6 December 1865]

Amendment XIV

Section 1. All persons born or naturalized in the United States and subject to the jurisdiction thereof, are citizens of the United States and of the State wherein they reside. No State shall make or enforce any law which shall abridge the privileges or immunities of citizens of the United States; nor shall any State deprive any person of life, liberty, or property, without due process of law; nor deny to any person within its jurisdiction the equal protection of the laws.

Section 2. Representatives shall be apportioned among the several States according to their respective numbers, counting the whole number of persons in each State, excluding Indians not taxed. But when the right to vote at any election for the choice of electors for President and Vice President of the United States, Representatives in Congress, the Executive and Judicial officers of a State, or the members of the Legislature thereof, is denied to any of the male inhabitants of such State, being twenty-one years of age, and citizens of the United States, or in any way abridged, except for participation in rebellion, or other crime, the basis of representation therein shall be reduced in the proportion which the number of such male citizens shall bear to the whole number of male citizens twenty-one years of age in such State.

Section 3. No person shall be a Senator or Representative in Congress, or elector of President and Vice President, or hold any office, civil or military, under the United States, or under any State, who, having previously taken an oath, as a member of Congress, or as an officer of the United States, or as a member of any State legislature, or as an executive or judicial officer of any State, to support the Constitution of the United States, shall have engaged in insurrection or rebellion against the same, or given aid or comfort to the enemies thereof. But Congress may by a vote of two-thirds of each House, remove such disability.

Section 4. The validity of the public debt of the United States, authorized by law, including debts incurred for payment of pensions and bounties for services in suppressing insurrection or rebellion, shall not be questioned. But neither the United States nor any State shall assume or pay any debt or obligation incurred in aid of insurrection or rebellion against the United States, or any claim for the loss or emancipation of any slave; but all such debts, obligations and claims shall be held illegal and void.

Section 5. The Congress shall have power to enforce, by appropriate legislation, the provisions of this article.

[Ratified 9 July 1868]

Amendment XV

Section 1. The right of citizens of the United States to vote shall not be denied or abridged by the United States or by any State on account of race, color, or previous condition of servitude.

Section 2. The Congress shall have power to enforce this article by appropriate legislation.

[Ratified 3 February 1870]

Amendment XVI

The Congress shall have power to lay and collect taxes on incomes, from whatever source derived, without apportionment among the several States, and without regard to any census or enumeration.

[Ratified 3 February 1913]

Amendment XVII

The Senate of the United States shall be composed of two Senators from each State, elected by the people thereof, for six years; and each Senator shall have one vote. The electors in each State shall have the qualifications requisite for electors of the most numerous branch of the State legislatures.

When vacancies happen in the representation of any State in the Senate, the executive authority of such State shall issue writs of election to fill such vacancies: *Provided,* That the legislature of any State may empower the executive thereof to make temporary appointments until the people fill the vacancies by election as the legislature may direct.

This amendment shall not be so construed as to affect the election or term of any Senator chosen before it becomes valid as part of the Constitution.

[Ratified 8 April 1913]

Amendment XVIII

Section 1. After one year from the ratification of this article the manufacture, sale, or transportation of intoxicating liquors within, the importation thereof into, or the exportation thereof from the United States and all territory subject to the jurisdiction thereof for beverage purposes is hereby prohibited.

Section 2. The Congress and the several States shall have concurrent power to enforce this article by appropriate legislation.

Section 3. This article shall be inoperative unless it shall have been ratified as an amendment to the Constitution by the legislatures of the several States, as provided in the Constitution, within seven years from the date of the submission hereof to the States by the Congress.

[Ratified 16 January 1919]

Amendment XIX

The right of citizens of the United States to vote shall not be denied or abridged by the United States or by any State on account of sex.

Congress shall have power to enforce this article by appropriate legislation.

[Ratified 18 August 1920]

Amendment XX

Section 1. The terms of the President and Vice President shall end at noon on the 20th day of January, and the terms of Senators and Representatives at noon on the 3d day of January, of the years in which such terms would have ended if this article had not been ratified; and the terms of their successors shall then begin

Section 2. The Congress shall assemble at least once in every year, and such meeting shall begin at noon on the 3d day of January, unless they shall by law appoint a different day.

Section 3. If, at the time fixed for the beginning of the term of the President, the President elect shall have died, the Vice President elect shall become President. If a President shall not have been chosen before the time fixed for the beginning of his term, or if the President elect shall have failed to qualify, then the Vice President elect shall act as President until a President shall have qualified; and the Congress may by law provide for the case wherein neither a President elect nor a Vice President elect shall have qualified, declaring who shall then act as President, or the manner in which one who is to act shall be selected, and such person shall act accordingly until a President or Vice President shall have qualified.

Section 4. The Congress may by law provide for the case of the death of any of the persons from whom the House of Representatives may choose a President whenever the right of choice shall have devolved upon them, and for the case of the death of any of the persons from whom the Senate may choose a Vice President whenever the right of choice shall have devolved upon them.

Section 5. Sections 1 and 2 shall take effect on the 15th day of October following the ratification of this article.

Section 6. This article shall be inoperative unless it shall have been ratified as an amendment to the Constitution by the legislatures of three-fourths of the several States within seven years from the date of its submission.

[Ratified 23 January 1933]

Amendment XXI

Section 1. The eighteenth article of amendment to the Constitution of the United States is hereby repealed.

Section 2. The transportation or importation into any State, Territory or possession of the United States for delivery or use therein of intoxicating liquors, in violation of the laws thereof, is hereby prohibited.

Section 3. This article shall be inoperative unless it shall have been ratified as an amendment to the Constitution by conventions in the several States, as provided in the Constitution, within seven years from the date of the submission hereof to the States by the Congress.

[Ratified 5 December 1933]

Amendment XXII

Section 1. No person shall be elected to the office of the President more than twice, and no person who has held the office of President, or acted as President, for more than two years of a term to which some other person was elected President shall be elected to the office of the President more than once. But this article shall not apply to any person holding the office of President when this Article was proposed by the Congress, and shall not prevent any person who may be holding the office of President, or acting as President, during the term within which this Article become[s] operative from holding the office of President or acting as President during the remainder of such term.

Section 2. This Article shall be inoperative unless it shall have been ratified as an amendment to the Constitution by the legislatures of three-fourths of the several States within seven years from the date of its submission to the States by the Congress.

[Ratified 27 February 1951]

Amendment XXIII

Section 1. The District constituting the seat of Government of the United States shall appoint in such manner as the Congress may direct:

A number of electors of President and Vice President equal to the whole number of Senators and Representatives in Congress to which the District would be entitled if it were a State, but in no event more than the least populous State; they shall be in addition to those appointed by the States, but they shall be considered, for the purposes of the election of President and Vice President, to be electors appointed by a State; and they shall meet in the District and perform such duties as provided by the twelfth article of amendment.

Section 2. The Congress shall have power to enforce this article by appropriate legislation.

[Ratified 29 March 1961]

Amendment XXIV

Section 1. The right of citizens of the United States to vote in any primary or other election for President or Vice President, for electors for President or Vice President, or for Senator or Representative in Congress, shall not be denied or abridged by the United States or any State by reason of failure to pay any poll tax or other tax.

Section 2. The Congress shall have power to enforce this article by appropriate legislation.

[Ratified 23 January 1964]

Amendment XXV

Section 1. In case of the removal of the President from office or of his death or resignation, the Vice President shall become President.

Section 2. Whenever there is a vacancy in the office of the Vice President, the President shall nominate a Vice President who shall take office upon confirmation by a majority vote of both Houses of Congress.

Section 3. Whenever the President transmits to the President pro tempore of the Senate and the Speaker of the House of Representatives his written declaration that he is unable to discharge the powers and duties of his office, and until he transmits to them a written declaration to the contrary, such powers and duties shall be discharged by the Vice President as Acting President.

Section 4. Whenever the Vice President and a majority of either the principal officers of the executive departments or of such other body as Congress may by law provide, transmit to the President pro tempore of the Senate and the Speaker of the House of Representatives their written declaration that the President is unable to discharge the powers and duties of his office, the Vice President shall immediately assume the powers and duties of the office as Acting President.

Thereafter, when the President transmits to the President pro tempore of the Senate and the Speaker of the House of Representatives his written declaration that no inability exists, he shall resume the powers and duties of his office unless the Vice President and a majority of either the principal officers of the executive department or of such other body as Congress may by law provide, transmit within four days to the President pro tempore of the Senate and the Speaker of the House of Representatives their written declaration that the President is unable to discharge the powers and duties of his office. Thereupon Congress shall decide the issue, assembling within forty-eight hours for that purpose if not in session. If the Congress, within twenty-one days after receipt of the latter written declaration, or, if Congress is not in session, within twenty-one days after Congress is required to assemble, determines by two-thirds vote of both houses that the President is unable to discharge the powers and duties of his office, the Vice President shall continue to discharge the same as Acting President; otherwise, the President shall resume the powers and duties of his office.

[Ratified 10 February 1967]

Amendment XXVI

Section 1. The right of citizens of the United States, who are eighteen years of age or older, to vote shall not be denied or abridged by the United States or by any State on account of age.

Section 2. The Congress shall have power to enforce this article by appropriate legislation.

[Ratified 1 July 1971]

Amendment XXVII

No law, varying the compensation for the services of the Senators and Representatives, shall take effect, until an election of Representatives shall have intervened.

[Ratified 7 May 1992]

APPENDIX B

❋ ❋ ❋ ❋ ❋ ❋ ❋

Justices of the Supreme Court

	Tenure	Appointed by	Replaced
JOHN JAY	1789–1795	Washington	
John Rutledge	1789–1791	Washington	
William Cushing	1789–1810	Washington	
James Wilson	1789–1798	Washington	
John Blair	1789–1796	Washington	
James Iredell	1790–1799	Washington	
Thomas Johnson	1791–1793	Washington	Rutledge
William Paterson	1793–1806	Washington	Johnson
JOHN RUTLEDGE	1795	Washington	Jay
Samuel Chase	1796–1811	Washington	Blair
OLIVER ELLSWORTH	1796–1800	Washington	Rutledge
Bushrod Washington	1798–1829	John Adams	Wilson
Alfred Moore	1799–1804	John Adams	Iredell
JOHN MARSHALL	1801–1835	John Adams	Ellsworth
William Johnson	1804–1834	Jefferson	Moore
Brockholst Livingston	1806–1823	Jefferson	Paterson
Thomas Todd	1807–1826	Jefferson	(new judgeship)
Gabriel Duval	1811–1835	Madison	Chase

Chief justices' names appear in capital letters.

	Tenure	Appointed by	Replaced
Joseph Story	1811–1845	Madison	Cushing
Smith Thompson	1823–1843	Monroe	Livingston
Robert Trimble	1826–1828	John Q. Adams	Todd
John McLean	1829–1861	Jackson	Trimble
Henry Baldwin	1830–1844	Jackson	Washington
James Wayne	1835–1867	Jackson	Johnson
ROGER B. TANEY	1836–1864	Jackson	Marshall
Phillip P. Barbour	1836–1841	Jackson	Duval
John Catron	1837–1865	Jackson	(new judgeship)
John McKinley	1837–1852	Van Buren	(new judgeship)
Peter V. Daniel	1841–1860	Van Buren	Barbour
Samuel Nelson	1845–1872	Tyler	Thompson
Levi Woodbury	1845–1851	Polk	Story
Robert C. Grier	1846–1870	Polk	Baldwin
Benjamin R. Curtis	1851–1857	Fillmore	Woodbury
John A. Campbell	1853–1861	Pierce	McKinley
Nathan Clifford	1858–1881	Buchanan	Curtis
Noah H. Swayne	1862–1881	Lincoln	McLean
Samuel F. Miller	1862–1890	Lincoln	Daniel
David Davis	1862–1877	Lincoln	Campbell
Stephen J. Field	1863–1897	Lincoln	(new judgeship)
SALMON CHASE	1864–1873	Lincoln	Taney
William Strong	1870–1880	Grant	Grier
Joseph P. Bradley	1870–1892	Grant	Wayne
Ward Hunt	1872–1882	Grant	Nelson
MORRISON R. WAITE	1874–1888	Grant	Chase
John Marshall Harlan	1877–1911	Hayes	Davis
William B. Woods	1880–1887	Hayes	Strong
Stanley Matthews	1881–1889	Garfield	Swayne
Horace Gray	1881–1902	Arthur	Clifford
Samuel Blatchford	1881–1893	Arthur	Hunt
Lucius Q. C. Lamar	1888–1893	Cleveland	Woods
MELVILLE W. FULLER	1888–1910	Cleveland	Waite
David J. Brewer	1889–1910	Harrison	Matthews

	Tenure	Appointed by	Replaced
Henry B. Brown	1890–1906	Harrison	Miller
George Shiras, Jr.	1892–1903	Harrison	Bradley
Howell E. Jackson	1893–1895	Harrison	Lamar
Edward D. White	1894–1910	Cleveland	Blatchford
Rufus W. Peckham	1895–1909	Cleveland	Jackson
Joseph McKenna	1898–1925	McKinley	Field
Oliver Wendell Holmes	1902–1932	T. Roosevelt	Gray
William R. Day	1903–1922	T. Roosevelt	Shiras
William H. Moody	1906–1910	T. Roosevelt	Brown
Horace H. Lurton	1909–1914	Taft	Peckham
Charles Evans Hughes	1910–1916	Taft	Brewer
EDWARD D. WHITE	1910–1921	Taft	Fuller
Willis Van Devanter	1910–1937	Taft	White
Joseph R. Lamar	1910–1916	Taft	Moody
Mahlon Pitney	1912–1922	Taft	Harlan
James McReynolds	1914–1941	Wilson	Lurton
Louis D. Brandeis	1916–1939	Wilson	Lamar
John H. Clarke	1916–1922	Wilson	Hughes
WILLIAM H. TAFT	1921–1930	Harding	White
George Sutherland	1922–1938	Harding	Clarke
Pierce Butler	1922–1939	Harding	Day
Edward T. Sanford	1923–1930	Harding	Pitney
Harlan F. Stone	1925–1941	Coolidge	McKenna
CHARLES EVANS HUGHES	1930–1941	Hoover	Taft
Owen J. Roberts	1930–1945	Hoover	Sanford
Benjamin N. Cardozo	1932–1938	Hoover	Holmes
Hugo L. Black	1937–1971	F. Roosevelt	Van Devanter
Stanley F. Reed	1938–1957	F. Roosevelt	Sutherland
Felix Frankfurter	1939–1962	F. Roosevelt	Cardozo
William O. Douglas	1939–1975	F. Roosevelt	Brandeis
Frank Murphy	1940–1949	F. Roosevelt	Butler
James F. Byrnes	1941–1942	F. Roosevelt	McReynolds

	Tenure	Appointed by	Replaced
HARLAN F. STONE	1941–1946	F. Roosevelt	Hughes
Robert H. Jackson	1941–1954	F. Roosevelt	Stone
Wiley B. Rutledge	1943–1949	F. Roosevelt	Byrnes
Harold H. Burton	1945–1958	Truman	Roberts
FRED M. VINSON	1946–1953	Truman	Stone
Tom C. Clark	1949–1967	Truman	Murphy
Sherman Minton	1949–1956	Truman	Rutledge
EARL WARREN	1953–1969	Eisenhower	Vinson
John M. Harlan	1955–1971	Eisenhower	Jackson
William J. Brennan	1956–1990	Eisenhower	Minton
Charles E. Whittaker	1957–1962	Eisenhower	Reed
Potter Stewart	1958–1981	Eisenhower	Burton
Byron R. White	1962–1993	Kennedy	Whittaker
Arthur J. Goldberg	1962–1965	Kennedy	Frankfurter
Abe Fortas	1965–1969	Johnson	Goldberg
Thurgood Marshall	1967–1991	Johnson	Clark
WARREN E. BURGER	1969–1986	Nixon	Warren
Harry A. Blackmun	1970–1994	Nixon	Fortas
Lewis F. Powell	1971–1987	Nixon	Black
William H. Rehnquist	1971–	Nixon	Harlan
John Paul Stevens	1975–	Ford	Douglas
Sandra Day O'Connor	1981–	Reagan	Stewart
WILLIAM H. REHNQUIST	1986–	Reagan	Burger
Antonin Scalia	1986–	Reagan	Rehnquist
Anthony M. Kennedy	1988–	Reagan	Powell
David H. Souter	1990–	Bush	Brennan
Clarence Thomas	1991–	Bush	Marshall
Ruth Bader Ginsburg	1993–	Clinton	White
Stephen Breyer	1994–	Clinton	Blackmun

INDEX

* * * * * * * * *

by Virgil Diodato